Math in Focus®

Singapore Math®
by Marshall Cavendish

Fact Fluency

Author
Susan Resnick

Course 1

marshall cavendish education

U.S. Distributor
Houghton Mifflin Harcourt.
The Learning Company™

Published by Marshall Cavendish Education
Times Centre, 1 New Industrial Road, Singapore 536196
Customer Service Hotline: (65) 6213 9688
US Office Tel: (1-914) 332 8888 | Fax: (1-914) 332 8882
E-mail: cs@mceducation.com
Website: www.mceducation.com

Distributed by
Houghton Mifflin Harcourt
125 High Street
Boston, MA 02110
Tel: 617-351-5000
Website: www.hmhco.com/programs/math-in-focus

First published 2020

ISBN 978-0-358-10519-0

Printed in Singapore

5 6 7 8 9 10 11 1401 29 28 27 26 25 24
4500881884 B C D E F

Contents

Chapter 6 Percent

Chapter 7 Algebraic Expressions

Chapter 8 Equations and Inequalities

Chapter 9 The Coordinate Plane

Chapter 10 Area of Polygons

Preface

This book is part of your **Math in Focus®** program.

Each practice in **Math in Focus®** ***Fact Fluency*** can be completed in about ten minutes.

This is what you will do in this book.

- Apply specific strategies in **Fact Builder** to promote fluency.
- Analyze problems and apply multiple problem-solving strategies in **Fact Strategy Practice**.
- Synthesize and apply your knowledge of fact strategies to real-world problems in **Apply and Build Knowledge**.
- Evaluate and create new mathematical thinking in **Writing about Math** through movement, drawing, writing, or talking.
- Prepare for future learning with more difficult problems in **Challenge Questions**.

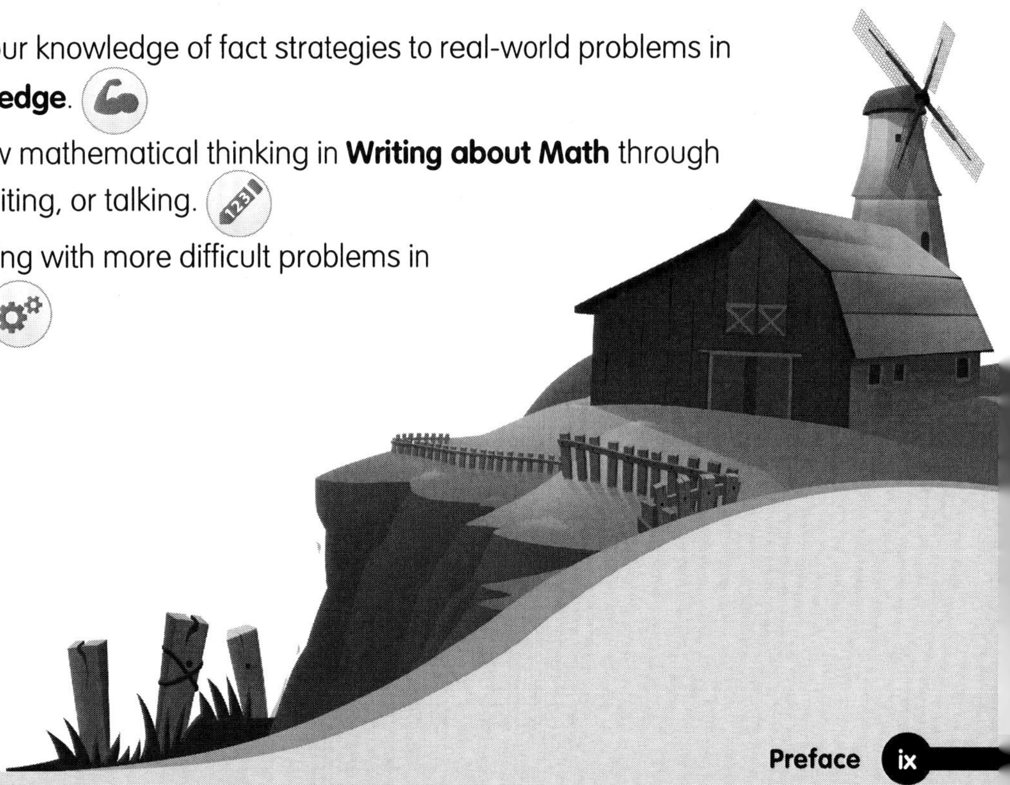

For Teachers and Parents

Math in Focus® ***Fact Fluency*** targets two critical elements of mathematical learning—conceptual understanding and fluency. Some activities focus on the understanding of grade-level skills and conceptual standards, while others focus on helping students achieve fluency expectations.

Activities in **Math in Focus®** ***Fact Fluency*** align to grade-level standards.

An Emphasis on Instruction

Students can be expected to complete each practice in **Math in Focus®** ***Fact Fluency*** in approximately ten minutes, making the practices useful as morning work, class openers, math center or station activities, and as homework.

Instructional Support

An Answer Key is available at the back of the book.

Name: ______________________ Date: ____________

Chapter 1 Fact Fluency

Whole Numbers, Prime Numbers, and Prime Factorization

1a One-Digit Multiplication

Find each missing product or factor.

1. $6 \times 7 =$ ______
2. $5 \times$ ______ $= 35$
3. $8 \times 9 =$ ______
4. $8 \times$ ______ $= 64$
5. $3 \times 9 =$ ______
6. $6 \times$ ______ $= 24$
7. $7 \times 8 =$ ______
8. $6 \times 6 =$ ______
9. $8 \times$ ______ $= 48$
10. $9 \times$ ______ $= 54$
11. $7 \times 7 =$ ______
12. $9 \times 9 =$ ______

Solve.

13. $9 \times 6 = (9 \times 1) + (9 \times$ ______ $)$
14. $9 \times 8 \times 7 = 7 \times 4 \times 2 \times 3 \times$ ______
15. What strategy did you use to solve 14?

______

______

1b One-Digit Division

Solve each problem as quickly as you can.

1. $72 \div 8 =$ ______
2. $72 \div 9 =$ ______
3. $64 \div 8 =$ ______
4. $54 \div 6 =$ ______
5. $42 \div 7 =$ ______
6. $24 \div 8 =$ ______
7. $81 \div 9 =$ ______
8. $49 \div 7 =$ ______
9. $48 \div 6 =$ ______
10. $56 \div 8 =$ ______
11. $32 \div 4 =$ ______
12. $63 \div 9 =$ ______
13. If $81 \div 9 \div 9 =$ ______, then $64 \div 8 \div 8 =$ ______.
14. Make up another problem that follows the pattern above:

______

1c Prime Numbers

A number is **prime** when it has exactly two **factors**, 1 and itself.
A number that is not prime is called **composite**.

Example

A number is divisible by

2	if it is even
3	if the sum of its digits is divisible by 3
4	if the last two digits are divisible by 4
5	if the last digit is a 5 or 0
6	if it is divisible by both 3 and 2
7	when the last digit is doubled and subtracted from the other digits and the result is 0 or divisible by 7
8	if the last three digits are divisible by 8
9	if the sum of its digits is divisible by 9

Use the divisibility rules to help you determine if a number is prime.

Is 1043 divisible by 7?

Double last digit: $3 \times 2 = 6$

Subtract from the other digits: $104 - 6 = 98$

$98 \div 7 = 14$

1043 is divisible by 7. So, 1043 is not a prime number.

Determine if each number is prime. Circle Prime or Composite. If the number is composite, identify the divisibility rule used to prove that it is not prime.

1. 37 Prime / Composite Rule: ____________________
2. 432 Prime / Composite Rule: ____________________
3. 3639 Prime / Composite Rule: ____________________
4. 1719 Prime / Composite Rule: ____________________
5. List the first 10 prime numbers.

   ____, ____, ____, ____, ____, ____, ____, ____, ____, ____,

Identify all of the divisibility rules that apply to each composite number.

6. 1428 ____________________
7. 7711 ____________________

1d Prime Factoring

You can **factor** a composite into the product of prime numbers.

First, try dividing by 2, 3, 5, or 7. Continue dividing until only prime numbers are left.

Example

Write 36 as a product of its prime factors.

Method 1: Factor Ladder

2	36
2	18
3	9
	3

Method 2: Factor Tree

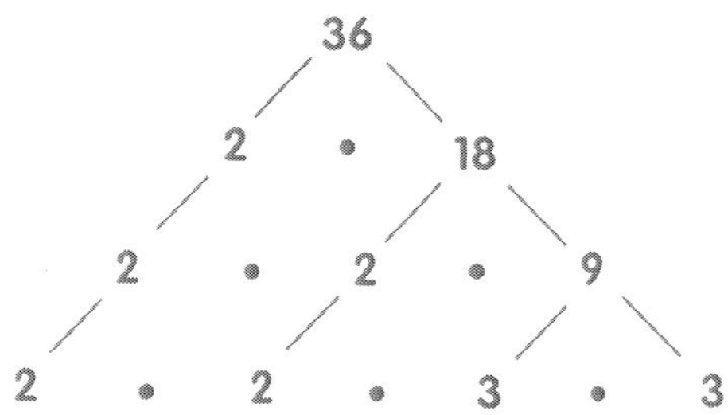

$36 = 2 \cdot 2 \cdot 3 \cdot 3$

1 Write 240 as a product of its prime factors. Choose one method to solve. Show your work.

2 Which method did you use in **1**? Why did you choose the method? How did it help?

____

____

____

1e More Practice on Prime Factoring

1. Match each composite number to its prime factors. Match the prime number to the word Prime.

729 •	• 2×197
181 •	• $3 \times 3 \times 47$
423 •	• $2 \times 41 \times 2$
394 •	• $3 \times 3 \times 3 \times 3 \times 3 \times 3$
164 •	• Prime

2. Did you notice some large prime factors in 1? How do you know they are prime factors?

____

____

1f Real-World Prime Number Problems

Cryptology is the science of writing and solving secret codes. Cryptologists often use prime numbers to encode data.

A sphenic number is the product of three different prime numbers.

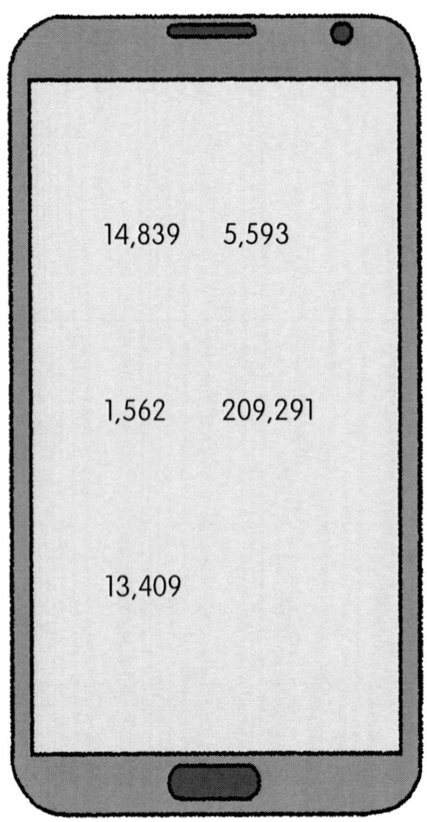

Use the sphenic numbers to crack the code in Aimee's text message to her son.

1. List the three prime factors of each sphenic number. Use a calculator to help you.

   14,839 = ______ × ______ × ______

   5,593 = ______ × ______ × ______

   1,562 = ______ × ______ × ______

   209,291 = ______ × ______ × ______

   13,409 = ______ × ______ × ______

2. Decode by replacing each prime factor with its letter in the code table below.
   (Hint: You may have to unscramble each set of 3 letters for the code to work.)

2	3	5	7	11	13	17	19	23	29	31
A	B	C	D	E	F	G	H	I	J	K
37	41	43	47	53	59	61	67	71	73	79
L	M	N	O	P	Q	R	S	T	U	V
83	89	97	101							
W	X	Y	Z							

Aimee's text message to her son is _ _ _   _ _ _   _ _ _   _ _ _   _ _ _.

1g Prime Factoring

Adam is setting up lights for a school dance. He wants all the lights to go on and off at different intervals. So, he sets the red light to flash every 2 seconds, the blue light every 3 seconds, the green light every 5 seconds and the white light every 7 seconds. He thinks his method will ensure that all four lights never flash at the same time.

Do you agree with Adam's thinking? Show your work to justify your answer.

Name: ______________________ Date: ______________

Chapter 2 Fact Fluency

Whole Numbers: Multiplication and Division

2a Mixed Multiplication and Division

Fill in the related facts.

1. $3 \times 7 =$ ______ $7 \times 3 =$ ______ ______ $\div 7 = 3$ ______ $\div 3 = 7$

2. ______ $\div 7 = 8$ ______ $\div 8 = 7$ ______ $\times 7 =$ ______

   ______ $\times 8 =$ ______

Use the related facts to help you solve.

3. $6 \times 8 =$ ______ so, $12 \times 8 =$ ______ and $3 \times 8 =$ ______.

4. $54 \div 9 =$ ______ so, $54 \div 18 =$ ______ and $540 \div 18 =$ ______.

5. How did the related facts help you solve these problems?

   ____

   ____

2b Mixed Multiplication and Division

Solve each problem as quickly as you can. Have a partner time you. **Time:** ______

1. $5 \times 8 =$ ______
2. $6 \times 7 =$ ______
3. $32 \div 8 =$ ______
4. $63 \div 7 =$ ______
5. $42 \div 6 =$ ______
6. $8 \times 7 =$ ______
7. $72 \div 9 =$ ______
8. $7 \times 3 =$ ______
9. $49 \div 7 =$ ______
10. $4 \times 8 =$ ______
11. $27 \div 3 =$ ______
12. $3 \times 6 =$ ______
13. Circle True or False. Explain and write an example to prove your thinking.

    $36 \times 6 = (30 \times 6) + (6 \times 6)$ True / False

    Explanation: ______________________________

    Example: ______________________________

2c Multi-Digit Multiplication and Division

Fill in each related fact.

1. $45 \times 3 =$ ______ $45 \times 30 =$ ______ $45 \times 33 =$ ______

2. $156 \times 6 =$ ______ $156 \times 70 =$ ______ $156 \times 76 =$ ______

Solve.

3. $\begin{array}{r} 164 \\ \times \quad 3 \\ \hline \end{array}$

4. $\begin{array}{r} 298 \\ \times \quad 34 \\ \hline \end{array}$

5. $\begin{array}{r} 345 \\ \times \quad 21 \\ \hline \end{array}$

6. $39 \div 3 =$ ______

7. $120 \div 6 =$ ______

8. $454 \div 2 =$ ______

9. $3\overline{)693}$

10. $9\overline{)729}$

11. $8\overline{)64{,}032}$

2d Multi-Digit Multiplication and Division

Solve. Show your work.

1. Sara is collecting canned food for a food drive. She collects 32 boxes of cans. Each box contains 45 cans. How many cans does she collect?

2. Each family must receive a minimum of 14 cans of food in their food bag. How many food bags can Sara fill?

3. In addition to the canned food, each food bag will need 4 packets of tuna, 2 boxes of cereal, and 3 bags of spaghetti. How many of each item will Sara need to complete the bags?

2e Order of Operations

Example

The order of operations tells us the order to solve an expression.

Solve $9 \times 6 + 12 \div 4$.

Step 1: Multiply

$9 \times 6 = 54$

Step 2: Divide

$12 \div 4 = 3$

Step 3: Add

$54 + 3 = 57$

$9 \times 6 + 12 \div 4 = 57$

Solve.

1. $(4 - 2) \times 7 + 3 =$ ____________

2. $8 \times 9 + 32 \div 8 =$ ____________

3. $21 + 19 - 12 \times 3 =$ ____________

4. $77 \div 11 + (33 \div 3) - 10 =$ ____________

2f Order of Operations

For each question, write ×, ÷, +, or – in the circle and use each symbol only once. Fill in the missing answers with the four numbers shown below.

14 30 60 11

1. (30 ◯ 50) – (40 ◯ 2) = ________
2. (42 ◯ 7 + 30) ◯ 6 = ________
3. (90 ◯ 10) ◯ 4 ◯ 2 = ________
4. 21 ◯ (9 ◯ 3) ◯ 10 = ________
5. Choose a number between 50 and 99. Write an expression using all the symbols (×, ÷, +, –) with the chosen number as the answer.

2g Real-World Order of Operations Problems

Solve. Show your work.

Matthew is shopping for a pair of jeans and a T-shirt at Big Discount Shop. A pair of black jeans costs $35 at the original price. A T-shirt costs $12.00 on sale. Matthew has a discount coupon of $15 for non-sale items and a discount coupon of $10 for the total price of his items. He cannot combine the discount coupons.

1. What is the least expensive way to buy the black jeans and the T-shirt? Which coupon should Matthew use? Show your work to justify your answer.

2 How much will Matthew have to pay if he uses the least expensive way?

3 Blue jeans are on sale for $32. Should Matthew buy the black jeans or the blue jeans if he wants to pay the least possible amount for the jeans and the T-shirt? Show your work to justify your answer.

2h Real-World Order of Operations Problems

Solve. Show your work.

Mr. Romero is taking his class on a field trip to the museum.

Mr. Romero has a budget of $360. He needs at least one adult for every 6 students on the field trip. He wants to take as many students as possible.

1 How many students and adults can Mr. Romero take on the field trip?

2 Write the expression to justify your answer in 1.

2i Order of Operations

When following a recipe, it is often important to carry out the steps in a specific order. For example, you need to add milk before baking the cake.

Write a list of steps for something you need to do in a specific order for it to work.

Name: ______________________ Date: ____________

Chapter 3 Fact Fluency
Fractions and Decimals

3a Finding Common Denominators

Fill in the missing numerator or denominator to complete each equivalent fraction.

1. $\frac{1}{2} = \frac{3}{\square} = \frac{\square}{8} = \frac{5}{\square} = \frac{\square}{100}$

2. $\frac{3}{9} = \frac{1}{\square} = \frac{2}{\square} = \frac{\square}{27} = \frac{30}{\square}$

3. $\frac{12}{18} = \frac{6}{\square} = \frac{2}{\square} = \frac{\square}{36} = \frac{4}{\square}$

Find the least common denominator for each pair of fractions.

Example

$\frac{1}{2}$ and $\frac{1}{4}$ Least common denominator is 4.

4. $\frac{1}{8}$ and $\frac{5}{16}$ Least common denominator is ____________.

5. $\frac{1}{2}$ and $\frac{1}{4}$ Least common denominator is ____________.

6. $\frac{2}{3}$ and $\frac{5}{6}$ Least common denominator is ____________.

7. $\frac{4}{5}$ and $\frac{6}{8}$ Least common denominator is ____________.

3b Adding and Subtracting Unlike Fractions

Example

$\frac{1}{2} + \frac{3}{4} =$ ________

$\frac{1}{2} = \frac{2}{4}$

Least common denominator is 4.

$\frac{1}{2} + \frac{3}{4} = \frac{2}{4} + \frac{3}{4}$

$= \frac{5}{4}$

Use the least common denominator to add or subtract the following fractions.

1. $\frac{1}{3} + \frac{1}{6} = \frac{\square}{6} + \frac{1}{6}$

   = ________

   = ________

2. $\frac{3}{5} + \frac{3}{10} = \frac{\square}{10} + \frac{3}{10}$

   = ________

3. $\frac{1}{4} + \frac{2}{8} =$ ________

4. $\frac{1}{3} + \frac{1}{2} =$ ________

5. $\frac{1}{3} + \frac{3}{5} =$ ________

6. $\frac{2}{7} + \frac{3}{8} =$ ________

7. $\frac{1}{3} - \frac{1}{5} =$ ________

8. $\frac{2}{3} - \frac{1}{2} =$ ________

9. $\frac{5}{7} - \frac{3}{6} =$ ________

10. $\frac{4}{6} - \frac{1}{4} =$ ________

3c Multiplying Fractions

Example

$\frac{3}{4} \times \frac{1}{3} = ?$

$\frac{3}{4} \times \frac{1}{3}$ means $\frac{3}{4}$ of $\frac{1}{3}$.

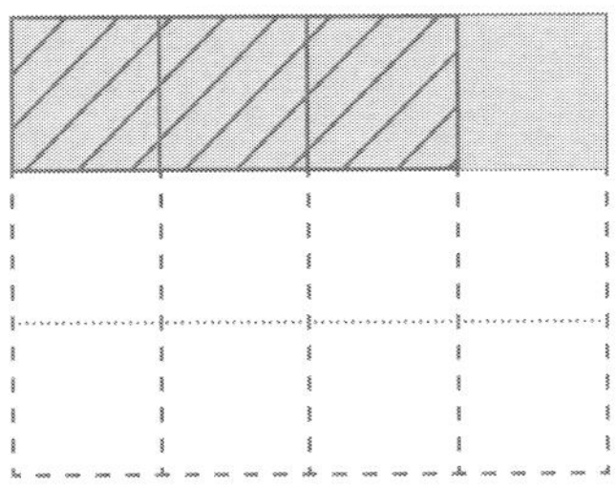

$\frac{3}{4} \times \frac{1}{3} = \frac{3}{12} = \frac{1}{4}$

Use models to help you multiply the fractions.

1. $\frac{2}{3} \times \frac{3}{4} =$ ____________

2. $\frac{1}{5} \times \frac{1}{2} =$ ____________

Solve.

3. $\frac{3}{4} \times \frac{2}{5} =$ ____________

4. $\frac{4}{20} \times \frac{1}{5} =$ ____________

5. $\frac{2}{7} \times \frac{1}{8} =$ ____________

6. $\frac{3}{9} \times \frac{1}{3} =$ ____________

7. $\frac{3}{8} \times \frac{1}{2} =$ ____________

8. $\frac{9}{30} \times \frac{3}{10} =$ ____________

3d Dividing Whole Numbers and Fractions

Example

$3 \div \frac{1}{2} = ?$

When reading $3 \div \frac{1}{2}$, think: "How many groups of $\frac{1}{2}$ are there in 3 wholes?"

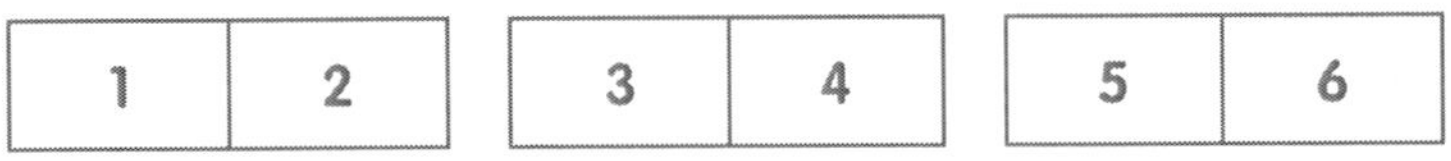

There are 6 groups of $\frac{1}{2}$ in 3 wholes.

$\frac{1}{2} \div 3 = ?$

When reading $\frac{1}{2} \div 3$, think: "When $\frac{1}{2}$ is divided into 3 pieces, how much of a whole is each piece?"

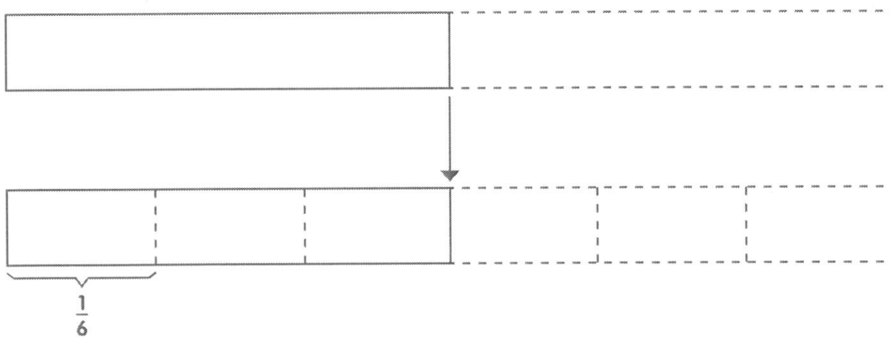

Each piece is $\frac{1}{6}$ of a whole.

Complete the models to help you divide.

1. $4 \div \frac{1}{3} =$ ______

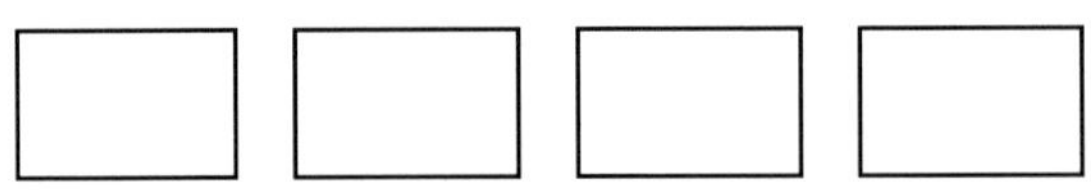

2. $3 \div \frac{1}{4} =$ ______

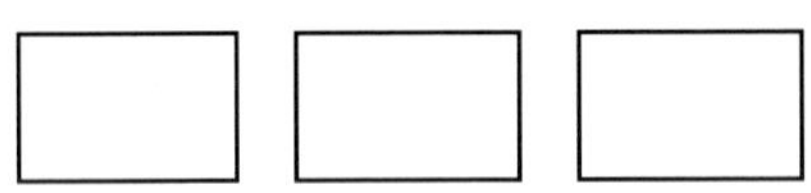

3. $\frac{1}{3} \div 4 =$ ______

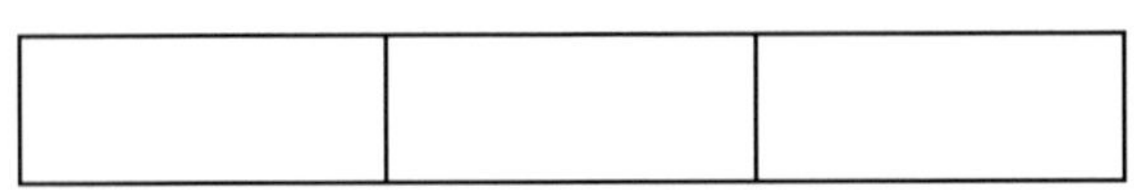

4. $\frac{2}{5} \div 3 =$ ______

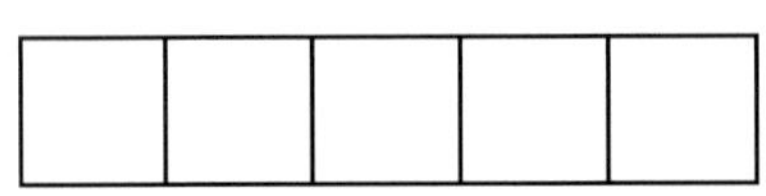

3e Dividing Whole Numbers and Fractions

Solve each problem as quickly as you can.

1. $3 \div \frac{1}{3} =$ ______ $6 \div \frac{1}{3} =$ ______ $9 \div \frac{1}{3} =$ ______

2. $\frac{1}{3} \div 3 =$ ______ $\frac{1}{3} \div 6 =$ ______ $\frac{1}{3} \div 9 =$ ______

3. $\frac{2}{3} \div 3 =$ ______ $\frac{2}{3} \div 6 =$ ______ $\frac{2}{3} \div 9 =$ ______

4. What pattern do you notice? How can this help you to solve other problems with division of fractions?

______

______

______

3f Dividing a Fraction by a Fraction

Example

$\frac{1}{2} \div \frac{1}{4} = ?$

Method 1:

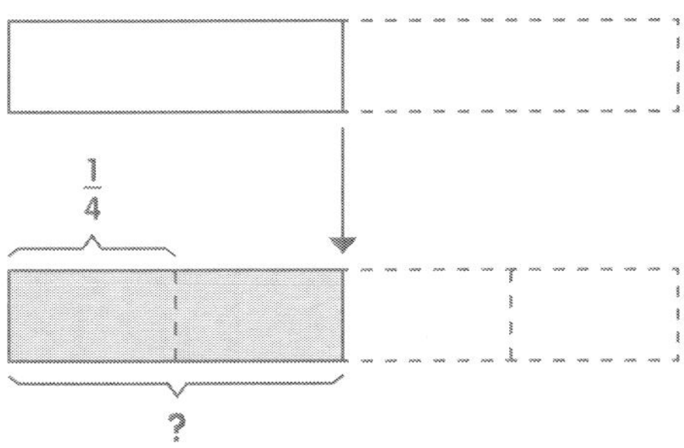

$\frac{1}{2} \div \frac{1}{4} = 2$

When reading $\frac{1}{2} \div \frac{1}{4}$, think: "How many groups of $\frac{1}{4}$ are there in $\frac{1}{2}$?"

Method 2:

$\frac{1}{2} \div \frac{1}{4} = \frac{1}{2} \times \frac{4}{1}$

$= \frac{4}{2}$

$= 2$

Division is the opposite of multiplication. When dividing fractions, you can multiply the first fraction by the reciprocal of the divisor.

Use both methods to solve the problem.

$\frac{3}{4} \div \frac{1}{2} =$ ____________

Method 1:	**Method 2:**

3g Dividing a Fraction by a Fraction

Solve.

1. $\frac{1}{4} \div \frac{1}{2} =$ ____________
2. $\frac{3}{8} \div \frac{1}{2} =$ ____________
3. $\frac{1}{2} \div \frac{5}{8} =$ ____________
4. $\frac{3}{4} \div \frac{2}{3} =$ ____________
5. $\frac{4}{7} \div \frac{1}{2} =$ ____________
6. $\frac{3}{14} \div \frac{1}{7} =$ ____________
7. $\frac{4}{6} \div \frac{2}{3} =$ ____________
8. $\frac{3}{4} \div \frac{1}{4} =$ ____________
9. $\frac{3}{9} \div \frac{1}{3} =$ ____________
10. What do you notice about the answers in the problems above? Write a rule that might help you predict the answer in the future.

____

____

____

3h Expressing Fractions as Decimals and Decimals as Fractions

Rewrite each fraction as a decimal.

Example

$\frac{1}{5} = \frac{2}{10}$

$= 0.2$

1. $\frac{9}{100} =$ ____________

2. $\frac{4}{5} =$ ____________

3. $\frac{7}{20} =$ ____________

4. $1\frac{1}{2} =$ ____________

5. $\frac{32}{10} =$ ____________

6. $\frac{3}{4} =$ ____________

Rewrite each decimal as a fraction in simplest form.

Example

$0.6 = \frac{6}{10}$

$= \frac{3}{5}$

7. 0.3 = ____________

8. 0.92 = ____________

9. 0.04 = ____________

10. 0.145 = ____________

11. 2.8 = ____________

12. 4.032 = ____________

3i Adding and Subtracting Decimals

Solve. Line up the decimal point correctly before you begin.

1. 4.5 + 3.2 = ________
2. 3.04 + 5.27 = ________
3. 13.14 – 12.95 = ________
4. 1.06 – 0.172 = ________

Find the missing digits.

5.
$$\begin{array}{r} 3\,.\,2\,4 \\ +\ \square\,.\,0\,\square \\ \hline 3\,.\,2\,7 \end{array}$$

6.
$$\begin{array}{r} 4\square\,.\,2\,4 \\ +\ 0\,.\,8\,9 \\ \hline 5\,0\,.\,1\,3 \end{array}$$

7.
$$\begin{array}{r} 1\,.\,0\,9\,4 \\ -\ 0\,.\,8\,9 \\ \hline 0\,.\,\square\,0\,4 \end{array}$$

8. Make your own missing digit subtraction problem.
Rule 1: The larger number must have the digit 4 in the hundredths place.
Rule 2: The smaller number must have at least 3 decimal places.

3j Multiplying Decimals

Example

$0.34 \times 0.2 = \frac{34}{100} \times \frac{2}{10}$

$= \frac{68}{1{,}000}$

$= 0.068$

Multiplying decimals is often easier in fraction form.
You can rewrite the decimal in fraction form and then multiply.
Finally, rewrite in decimal form.

Solve.

1. $0.4 \times 0.5 = \frac{4}{10} \times \frac{5}{\square}$

$= \frac{\square}{\square}$

= ________

2. $0.12 \times 5.4 = \frac{\square}{\square} \times \frac{\square}{\square}$

$= \frac{\square}{\square}$

= ________

3. $3.4 \times 0.09 = \frac{34}{10} \times \frac{9}{100}$

$= \frac{\square}{\square}$

= ________

4. $0.92 \times 0.03 = \frac{\square}{\square} \times \frac{\square}{\square}$

$= \frac{\square}{\square}$

= ________

3k Dividing Decimals

Example

$$0.048 \div 0.02 = \frac{48}{1,000} \div \frac{2}{100}$$
$$= \frac{48}{1,000} \times \frac{100}{2}$$
$$= \frac{4,800}{2,000}$$
$$= \frac{2,400}{1,000}$$
$$= 2.4$$

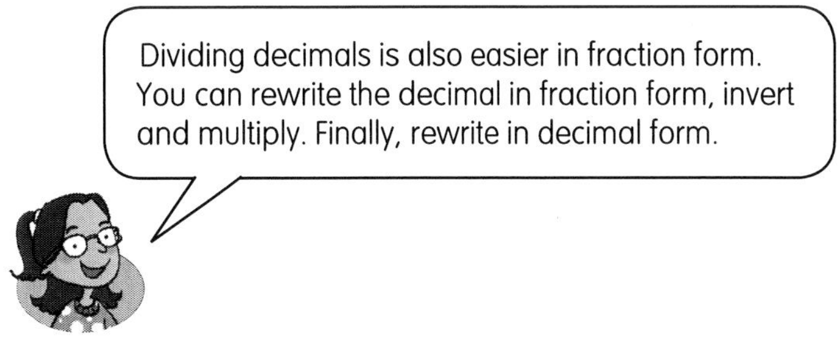

Write each decimal as a fraction.

1. $0.34 = \frac{\square}{\square}$
2. $0.043 = \frac{\square}{\square}$
3. $6.7 = \frac{\square}{\square}$

Divide. Express each answer in simplest form.

Example

$$\frac{2}{100} \div \frac{3}{10} = \frac{2}{100} \times \frac{10}{3}$$
$$= \frac{20}{300}$$
$$= \frac{1}{15}$$

4. $\frac{2}{10} \div \frac{4}{100} = \frac{2}{10} \times \frac{\square}{\square}$

   = ____________

5. $\frac{3}{100} \div \frac{15}{100} =$

6. $\frac{6}{10} \div \frac{4}{1,000} =$

Solve.

7. $0.32 \div 0.04 =$ ____________
8. $0.75 \div 0.5 =$ ____________
9. $0.042 \div 0.03 =$ ____________

31 Multiplying and Dividing Decimals

Complete the triangles by multiplying or dividing. Use fraction form to help you.

Example

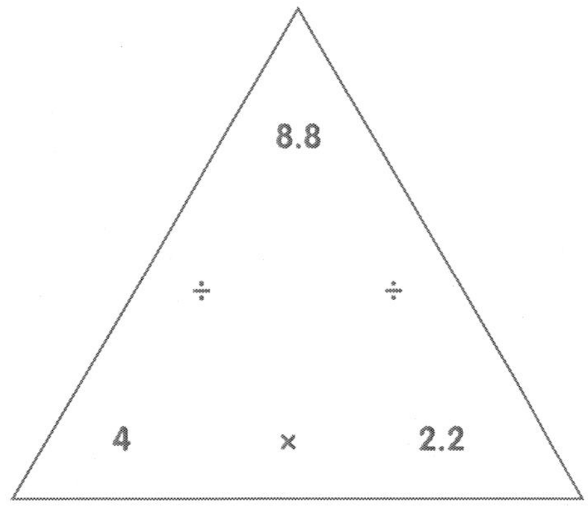

1

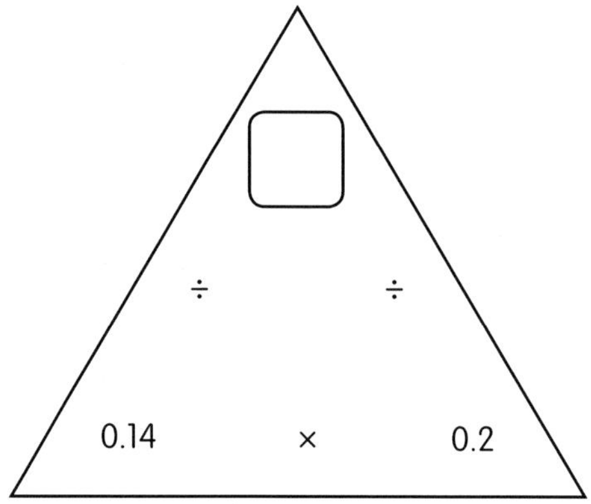

2

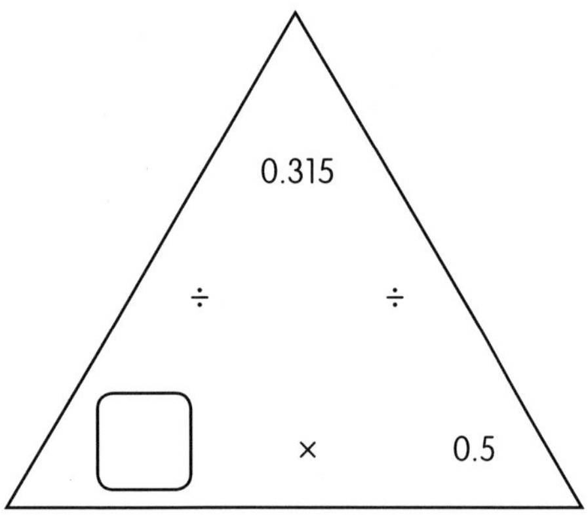

3

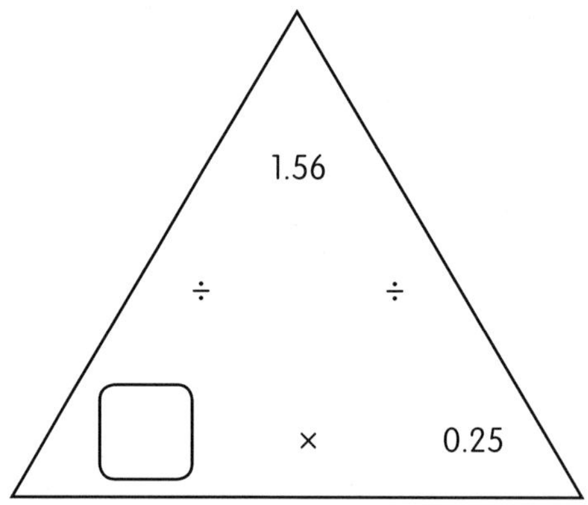

4

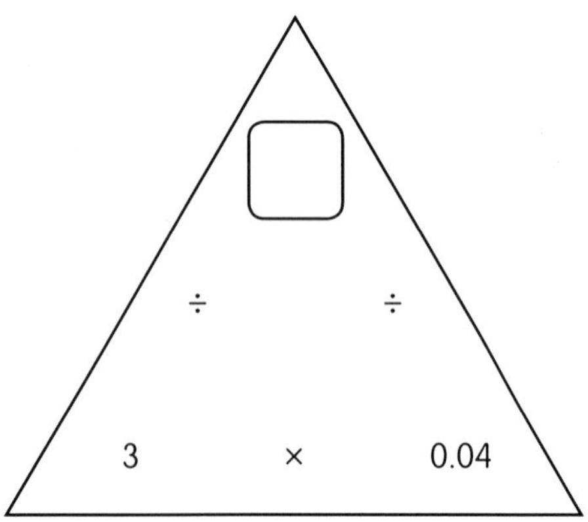

5

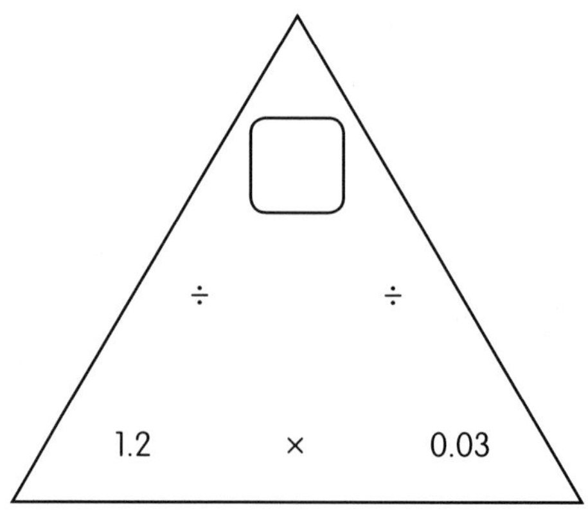

3m Real-World Fraction and Decimal Problems

For his science fair project, Javier studied plant growth under different conditions.

Plant A, which was exposed to music, grew 10.48 cm more than Plant B which was not.

Plant C, which was given nutrients, grew $4\frac{1}{2}$ cm more than Plant D which was not.

Plant D was $\frac{2}{3}$ of the height of Plant B.

Plant C was 14.98 cm tall.

Use the information provided to find the height of each plant. Label each plant according to the information given, then label their heights.

Plant ________	Plant ________	Plant ________	Plant ________
Height: ________ cm	Height: ________ cm	Height: ________ cm	Height: ________ cm

3n Fractions and Decimals

$$\frac{1}{2} + 0.4 + \frac{3}{5} + \left(\frac{2}{5} \times \frac{4}{10}\right) + \left(0.2 \times \frac{1}{3}\right) = ?$$

Zachary and Grace are discussing how to solve the above problem.

Zachary: "We should rewrite all fractions as decimals because it is easier to add decimals in the end."

Grace: "I disagree because $\frac{1}{3}$ makes it difficult. We should rewrite all decimals as fractions. Then, we can simplify the fractions."

1. Who do you think has a better argument?

___

2. Explain your thinking.

___

___

___

3. Solve using Zachary's or Grace's strategy.

Name: ______________________ Date: ______________

Chapter 4

Fact Fluency
Ratio

4a Finding Equivalent Fractions by Multiplication

Circle the fractions that are equivalent to the fraction in the box.

1. $\boxed{\frac{3}{4}}$ $\frac{6}{8}$ $\frac{5}{20}$ $\frac{9}{12}$ $\frac{12}{20}$ $\frac{75}{100}$ $\frac{30}{40}$

2. $\boxed{\frac{2}{5}}$ $\frac{4}{9}$ $\frac{4}{10}$ $\frac{16}{40}$ $\frac{18}{20}$ $\frac{40}{100}$ $\frac{800}{2,000}$

3. $\boxed{\frac{22}{25}}$ $\frac{88}{100}$ $\frac{44}{50}$ $\frac{11}{15}$ $\frac{166}{175}$ $\frac{40}{100}$ $\frac{3,520}{4,000}$

Write three equivalent fractions for each given fraction.

4. $\frac{1}{3}$ ____________, ____________, ____________

5. $\frac{6}{10}$ ____________, ____________, ____________

4b Simplifying Fractions by Division

Divide until you find the simplest form. Then, circle it.
(Hint: You may not need all of the lines.)

1. $\frac{100}{400}$ ______ ______ ______ ______ ______ ______

2. $\frac{24}{60}$ ______ ______ ______ ______ ______ ______

3. $\frac{575}{6,250}$ ______ ______ ______ ______ ______ ______

4c More Practice on Multiplication and Division of Fractions

1 Each brick is the product of the two bricks below it. Fill in the missing fractions to build the pyramid. Use a calculator to help you.

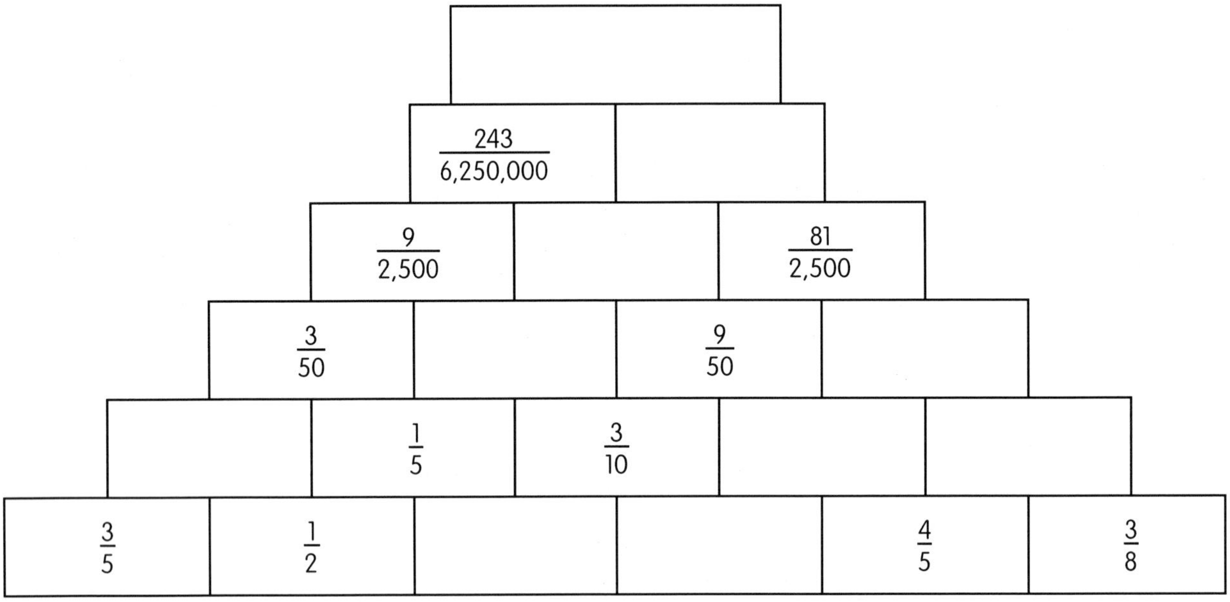

2 Make two observations about the pyramid.

____

____

____

____

____

4d Comparing Ratios

Example

There are 3 dogs to 4 cats.

The ratio of the number of dogs to the number of cats is **3 : 4**.

The ratio of the number of cats to the number of dogs is **4 : 3**.

You can compare two amounts using ratios.

Use the picture to answer the following questions.

1. What is the ratio of the number of grey cubes to the number of black cubes? __________

2. What is the ratio of the number of black cubes to the number of grey cubes? __________

3. What is the ratio of the number of grey cubes to the total number of cubes? __________

4e Finding Equivalent Ratios

Example

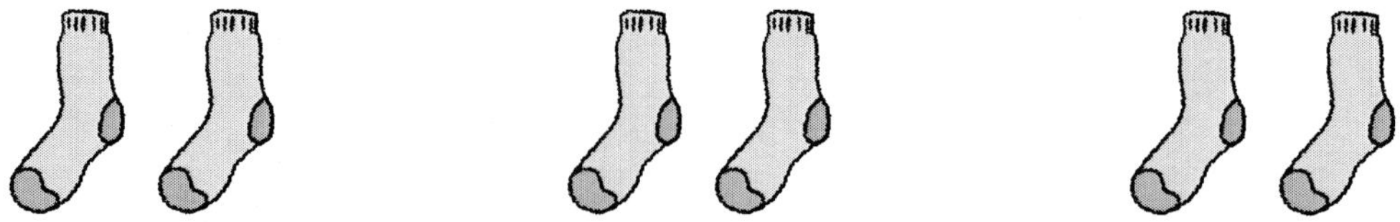

The ratio of the number of socks to the number of skirts is 6 : 3.

For every 2 socks, there is 1 skirt.

The ratio of the number of socks to the number of skirts is 2 : 1.

6 : 3 and **2 : 1** are equivalent ratios because they describe the same relationship.

Use the picture to find the equivalent ratios.

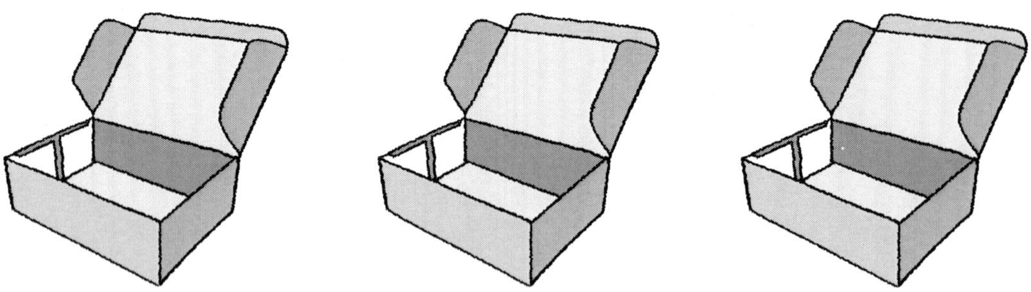

1. Find the ratio of the number of cupcakes to the number of boxes. ____________ : 3

2. Express the ratio of the number of cupcakes to the number of boxes in simplest form. ____________ : 1

3. Write two equivalent ratios that describe the relationship between the cupcakes and the boxes.

____________ and ____________

4f Equivalent Ratios

Find the equivalent ratios.

1. 4 : 8 = ________ : 2
2. 3 : 12 = 1 : ________
3. 25 : ________ = 1 : 3

Write the first three ratios equivalent to the given ratio.

4. 1 : 3 = ________ : ________, ________ : ________, and ________ : ________
5. 2 : 5 = ________ : ________, ________ : ________, and ________ : ________

Express each ratio in simplest form.

6. 125 : 5

   ________ : ________

7. 128 : 64

   ________ : ________

8. 350 : 150

   ________ : ________

9. What are the two methods for finding equivalent ratios?

____

____

4g Equivalent Ratios

Ryan lists the books in his class library below.

Fiction : Non-fiction
5 : 3
Biography: Fiction
2 : 10
Total number of fiction, biography and non-fiction books = 360

1. Draw a model to help you find the number of each type of book in the class library.

2. How many fiction books are there? ________

3. How many non-fiction books are there? ________

4. How many biographies are there? ________

4h Measurement Conversion

Jack is making soup for a party. See a part of his recipe below.

2 tablespoons of olive oil
10 tablespoons of coconut milk
32 ounces of chicken stock
2 cups of water

He has only a teaspoon to measure his liquid ingredients. Use the conversion table below to help Jack measure each liquid ingredient.

Cups	Fluid ounces	Tablespoons	Teaspoons
1	8	16	48
$\frac{3}{4}$	6	12	36
$\frac{1}{2}$	4	8	24
$\frac{1}{4}$	2	4	12

Example

Jack needs 1 tablespoon of honey for tea.

How many teaspoons of honey does Jack need?

Tablespoons : Teaspoons

÷ 4   4 : 12   ÷ 4

1 : 3

Jack needs 3 teaspoons of honey.

Jack needs ____________ teaspoons of olive oil, ____________ teaspoons of coconut milk, ____________ teaspoons of chicken stock, and ____________ teaspoons of water.

4i Ratio and Measurement

Harinah wants to redecorate her bedroom. She decides to make a scale model to try out her design.

1. The scale of her actual bedroom furniture to the model furniture is 24 : 1.
Use the dimensions of the actual furniture to calculate the dimensions of each model.

Furniture	Actual Dimensions in Inches	Model Dimensions in Inches
Bed	36×72	
Desk	48×30	
Chair	24×24	
Cupboard	96×144	
Bookshelf	12×12	

2. Choose one of the pieces of furniture in Harinah's room and sketch the model on the grid below.

Actual dimensions: ____________ × ____________

Model dimensions: ____________ × ____________

4j Ratio and Bar Model

1. Make up a real-world ratio problem that uses the bar model below.

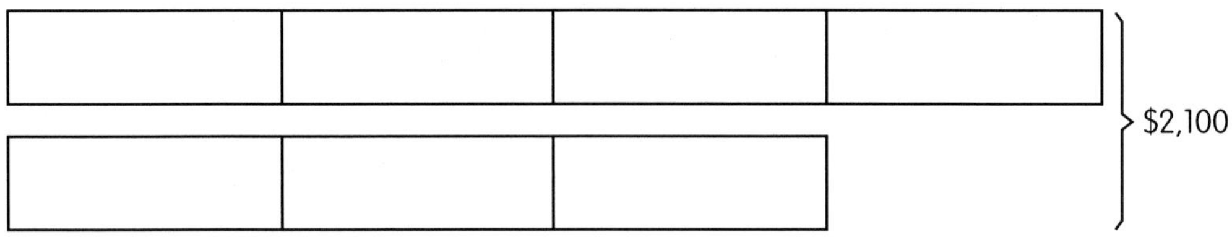

____

____

____

2. Solve the ratio problem. Show your work.

4k Ratio

Jonathan says sometimes a ratio can be written as a fraction; other times it cannot.

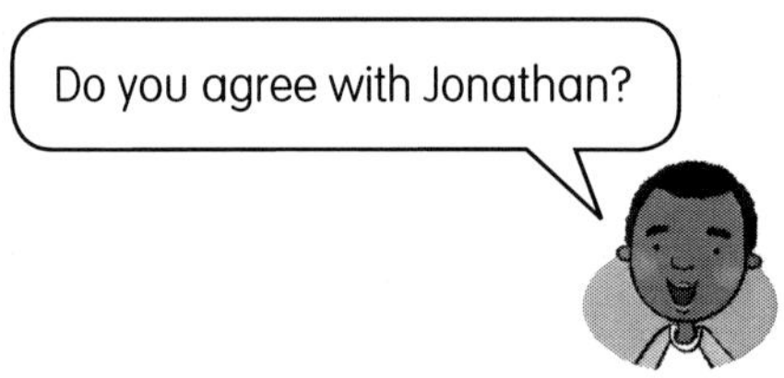

Give a specific example to justify your answer.

____

____

____

____

Name: ______________________ Date: ______________

Chapter 5 Fact Fluency

Rates

5a Fraction of a Set

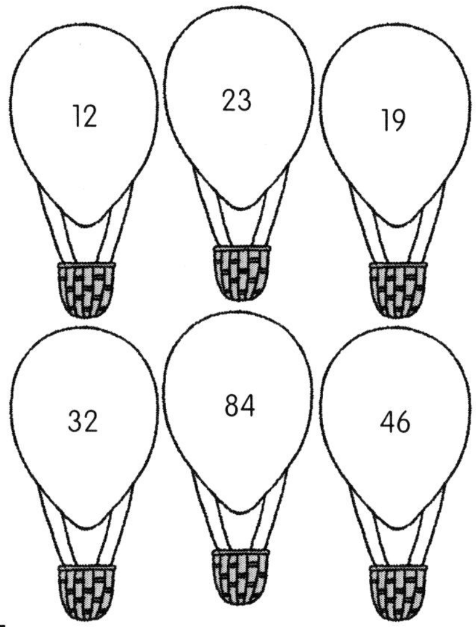

Use the picture to answer each question.

1. What fraction of the balloons have even numbers? ____________
2. What fraction of the balloons have prime numbers? ____________
3. What fraction of the balloons have numbers that are divisible by 7? ____________
4. What fraction of the balloons have numbers that are multiples of the number on another balloon? ____________
5. What fraction of the balloons have two-digit numbers? ____________

5b More Practice on Dividing Whole Numbers and Fractions

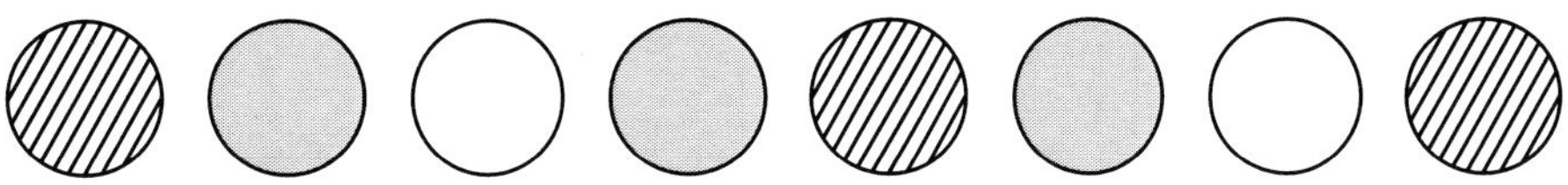

Use the picture to answer each question.

1. What fraction of the circles are striped? ____________ are white? ____________ are shaded? ____________
2. How many halves can you make from all the shaded circles? ____________
3. Write a division sentence for your answer in 2. ____________ ÷ ____________ = ____________
4. How many thirds can you make from all the white circles? ____________
5. Write a division sentence for your answer in 4. ____________ ÷ ____________ = ____________
6. If you only had $\frac{1}{2}$ of a circle, how many fourths can you make? ____________
7. How many thirds can you make from $\frac{1}{2}$ of the circle? ____________

5c More Practice on Dividing Whole Numbers and Fractions

Solve.

1. $5 \div \frac{1}{3} =$
2. $5 \div \frac{2}{3} =$
3. $\frac{1}{5} \div \frac{2}{3} =$
4. $6 \div \frac{1}{5} =$
5. $6 \div \frac{3}{5} =$
6. $\frac{3}{5} \div 6 =$
7. $3 \div \frac{1}{15} =$
8. $3 \div \frac{7}{15} =$
9. $\frac{7}{15} \div 3 =$

5d What is Rate?

Example

John takes 15 minutes to work on 5 math problems.

His rate is **15 minutes per 5 math problems** or **15 min/5 math problems.**

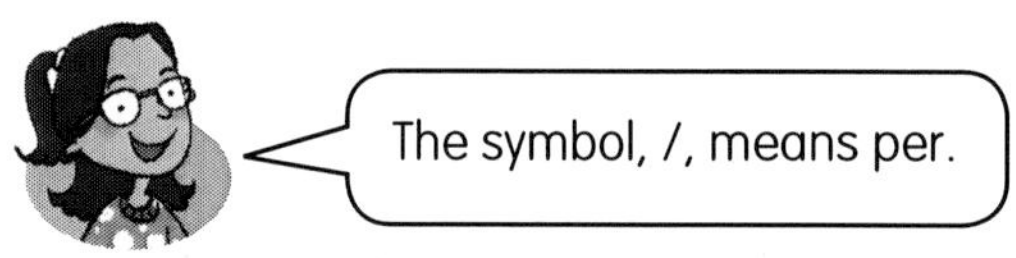

1. If John uses the same amount of time on each math problem, how long does it take for John to work on one problem? ____________

2. How would you describe the concept of unit rate?

____

____

3. How are rate and ratio the same? How are they different?

____

____

____

5e Finding a Unit Rate

Example

Ryan bought 5 apples for $10. What was the cost per apple?

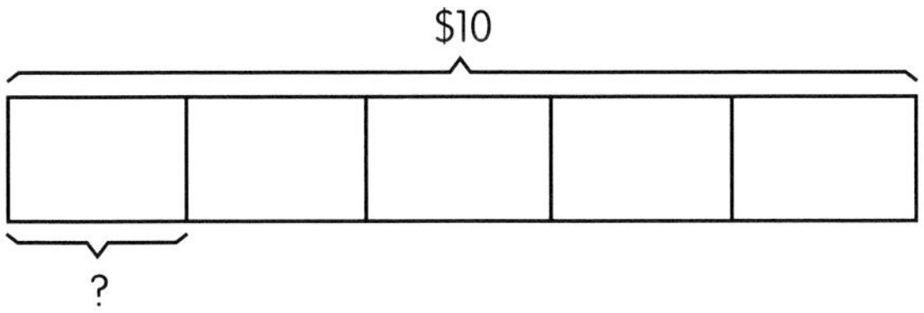

5 apples → $10

1 apple → $\frac{\$10}{5} = \frac{\$2}{1} = \$2$

From the bar model, each unit represents $2.
So, the unit rate is $2/apple or $2 per unit.

Find the unit rate.

1. Alexa buys 12 cupcakes for $6. The unit rate is $ ____________ per cupcake.
2. Noah drives 60 miles in 2 hours. His unit rate is ____________ miles per hour.
3. Maya takes 24 minutes to run 3 miles. Her unit rate is ____________ minutes per mile.
4. Mr. Brown pays $50.25 for 5 hats. The unit cost is $ ____________ per hat.

5f Finding a Unit Rate

Jayla was trying to buy the least expensive brand of rice.

1. Complete the table to determine the least expensive brand of rice in terms of price per ounce. (Hint: There are 16 ounces in a pound.) Round your answer to the nearest cent. Use a calculator to help you.

Brand of rice	Cost in dollars	Size of bag	Price per ounce
Cousin Ben	$4.39	15.8 ounces	
60-Second	$4.99	28 ounces	
Silver Star	$9.00	5 pounds	
Trademark Kitchen	$5.59	4 pounds	

2. Which brand was the least expensive in terms of price per ounce?

____

____

3. Did the answer surprise you? Explain your thinking.

____

____

5g Finding Rate with Formula

Example

Carlos biked 60 miles in 5 hours.
His rate is 60 miles/5 hours.
His unit rate is 12 miles/hour.

Finding Distance
Distance = Unit rate × Time
= 12 × 5
= 60 miles

Finding Time
Time = Distance ÷ Unit rate
= 60 ÷ 12
= 5 hours

You can also use this formula to find rate:

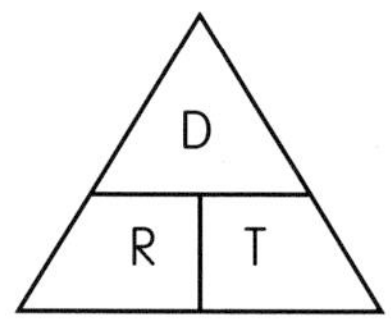

Rate = Distance ÷ Time
From the triangle, you can find distance and time.
Distance = Rate × Time
Time = Distance ÷ Rate

Solve using the formula.

1. Haley's house is 4.8 miles away from school. It takes her 24 minutes to ride to school. At what rate does she ride her bike? ____________ miles/min

2. She rides home at a rate of 0.3 miles/min from school. How long does it take her to get home? ____________ minutes

5h Finding Rate with Formula

In a women's triathlon, each contestant ran 13.1 miles, swam 1.2 miles, and biked 56 miles. Find the time each contestant took to complete each event. Round your answer to the nearest minute. Use a calculator to help you.

1.

Contestant	Event	Rate in miles per minute	Time in minutes
Emma	Running	0.32	
Kayla	Running	0.34	
Paige	Running	0.31	
Emma	Swimming	0.05	
Kayla	Swimming	0.03	
Paige	Swimming	0.04	
Emma	Biking	0.56	
Kayla	Biking	0.60	
Paige	Biking	0.61	

2. Who won the running portion of the triathlon? ____________

   What was her time? ____________

3. Who was winning after the first two events? ____________

4. Who won overall? ____________ What was her total time? ____________

5i Multiplying Decimals

Express each decimal as a fraction and multiply. Then, express your answer as a decimal.

Example

$0.4 \times 0.5 = \frac{4}{10} \times \frac{5}{10}$

$= \frac{20}{100}$

$= 0.2$

1. $0.2 \times 0.7 =$ ____________ $\times$ ____________

   $= \frac{\square}{100}$

   $=$ ____________

2. $0.04 \times 0.5 =$ ____________ $\times$ ____________

   $= \frac{\square}{1{,}000}$

   $=$ ____________

3. $1.2 \times 0.7 =$ ____________ $\times$ ____________

   $= \frac{\square}{\square}$

   $=$ ____________

Solve.

4. $0.12 \times 0.3 =$

5. $0.4 \times 0.01 =$

6. $1.3 \times 4.5 =$

7. $20.2 \times 0.34 =$

8. $0.003 \times 7 =$

9. $12 \times 1.009 =$

5j Dividing Decimals

The center number in the shape is the result from multiplying its opposite sides. Solve each puzzle.

Example

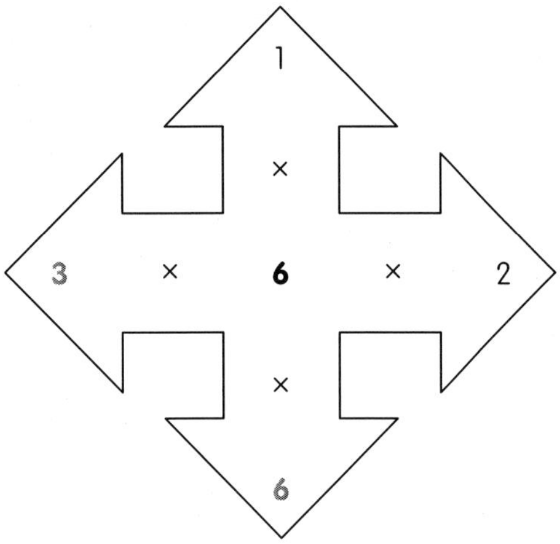

1

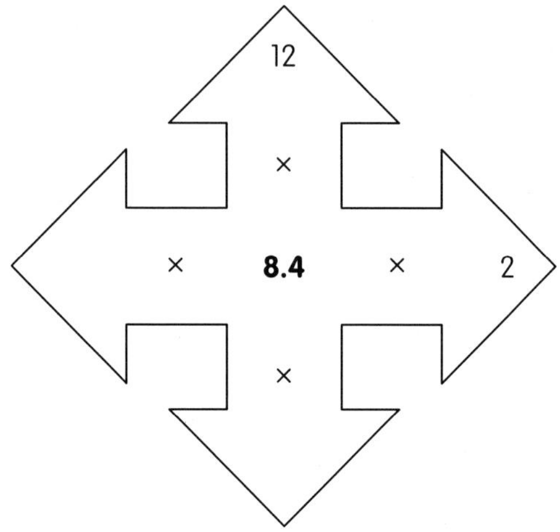

2

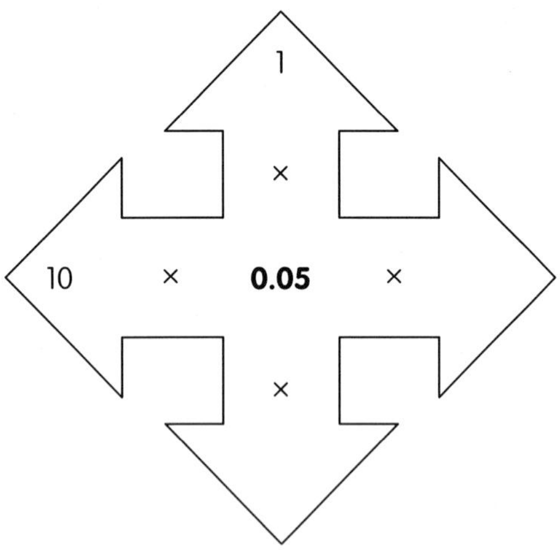

3

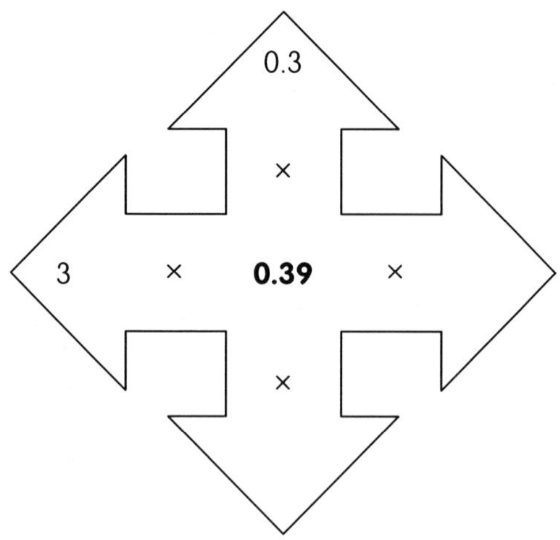

5k Finding Average Rate

It is easy to calculate rate when a car is moving at the same speed for the whole trip.

In the real world, cars will speed up, slow down, and stop at different parts of the trip.

How do you calculate the rate of a car that isn't moving at a constant speed?

You can calculate the average rate.

$$\text{Average rate} = \frac{\text{Total distance}}{\text{Total time}}$$

Jenna drove to visit her grandmother. She drove the first 10 miles in 20 minutes. Then, she reached the highway and drove the next 35 miles in 30 minutes.
(Hint: Convert minutes to hours before calculating average rate.)

1. What was the total distance Jenna drove? ____________ miles
2. What was her total time? ____________ minutes
3. What was Jenna's average rate in mph? ____________ miles/hour

mph means miles per hour

5l Real-World Average Rate Problems

Genevieve kept a log of her drives to visit some National Parks and landmarks. She started at the Grand Canyon.

Destination	Drive Time	Distance from previous location
Grand Canyon, AZ		0 miles
Bryce Canyon National Park, UT	4 h 30 min	262 miles
Craters of the Moon National Monument and Preserve, ID	8 h 30 min	504 miles
Yellowstone National Park, WY	4 h 45 min	235 miles
Glacier National Park, MT	6 h 15 min	376 miles

Use Genevieve's log above to find her average rate for the trip. Show your work.

5m Average Speed

An airplane travels 1,040 feet at 65 mph along the runway. It then takes off and travels 1,910 feet at 300 mph to its cruising altitude. It then travels for 1,631 miles in the air at 564 mph. On its descent, the airplane travels for 2,000 feet at 250 mph and then for 1,000 feet at 65 mph when landing.
(Hint: 5,280 feet = 1 mile)

1. Draw a diagram of the flight to show the trip.

2. How would you calculate the average speed of the airplane during the trip?

3. What is the average speed? Round to the nearest tenth. Use a calculator to help you.

Name: ______________________ Date: ______________

Chapter 6

Fact Fluency
Percent

6a Dividing by 10, 100, and 1,000

Solve each problem as quickly as you can.

1. $60 \div 10 =$ 6
2. $60 \div 100 =$ .6
3. $60 \div 1{,}000 =$ .06
4. $5.6 \div 10 =$ .56
5. $5.6 \div 100 =$ .056
6. $5.6 \div 1{,}000 =$ .0056
7. $0.34 \div 10 =$ .034
8. $34 \div 100 =$ .0034
9. $340 \div 1{,}000 =$ .00034
10. $200 \div 10 =$ 20
11. $200 \div 100 =$ 2.0
12. $200 \div 1{,}000 =$ .20

6b Finding Equivalent Fractions

Find the fractions that are equivalent to the fraction in the box.

1. $\boxed{\frac{2}{5}}$ $\frac{\boxed{4}}{10}$ $\frac{\boxed{10}}{25}$ $\frac{\boxed{40}}{100}$
2. $\boxed{\frac{4}{8}}$ $\frac{\boxed{10}}{20}$ $\frac{\boxed{25}}{50}$ $\frac{\boxed{50}}{100}$
3. $\boxed{\frac{3}{12}}$ $\frac{\boxed{1}}{4}$ $\frac{\boxed{5}}{20}$ $\frac{\boxed{25}}{100}$
4. $\boxed{\frac{3}{100}}$ $\frac{\boxed{.03}}{1}$ $\frac{\boxed{1.5}}{50}$ $\frac{\boxed{.3}}{10}$

6c Percent

Example

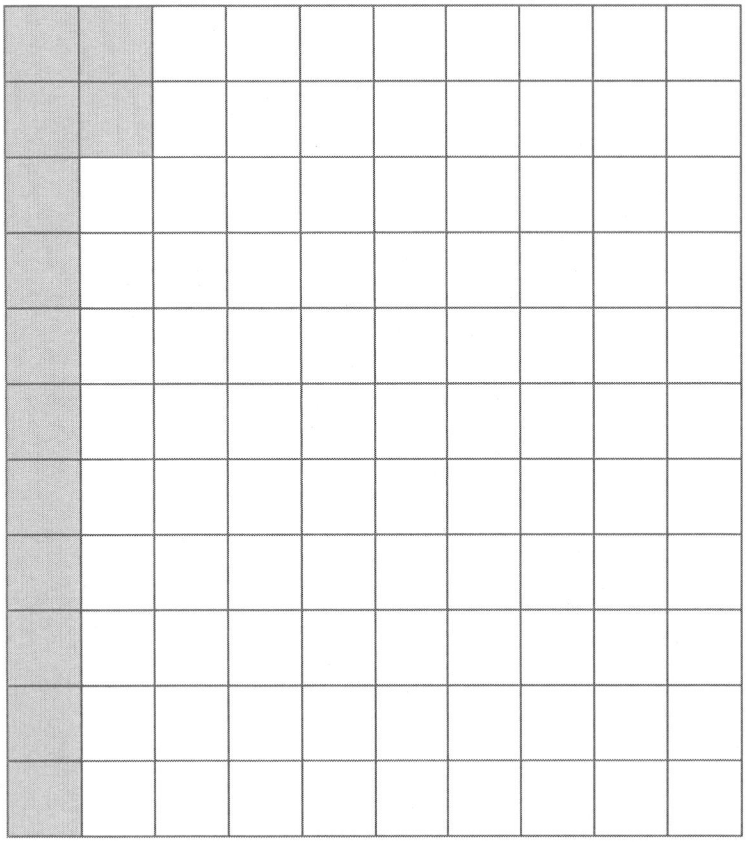

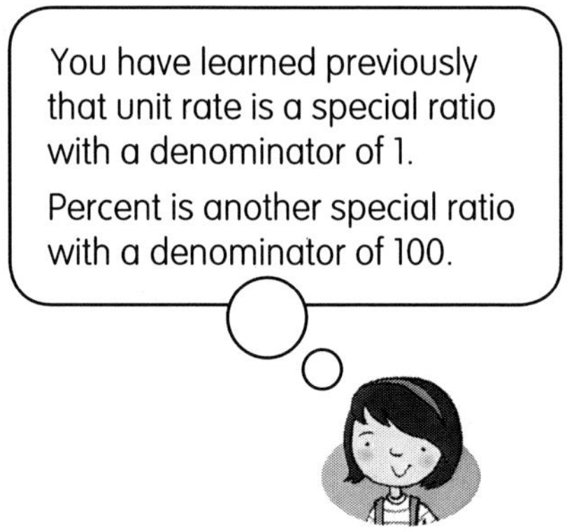

$\frac{12}{100}$ = **12 percent or 12%**

Express each fraction as a percent.

1. $\frac{3}{100}$ = 3 %
2. $\frac{34}{100}$ = 34 %
3. $\frac{78}{100}$ = 78 %
4. $\frac{13}{100}$ = 13 %
5. $\frac{20}{100}$ = 20 %
6. $\frac{1}{100}$ = 1 %

Express each percent as a fraction in simplest form.

7. 32% = ______
8. 14% = ______
9. 5% = ______

6d Finding Percents from Decimals

Example

Express 0.15 as a percent.

$0.15 = \frac{15}{100}$

$= 15\%$

First, express the decimal in fraction form with a denominator of 100. Then, express the fraction as a percent.

Complete the table.

Decimal Form	Fraction Form	Percent Form
0.56	$\frac{56}{100}$	56
0.08	$\frac{8}{100}$	8%
.17	$\frac{17}{100}$	17%
1.2	$\frac{120}{1000}$	120%

6e Finding Percent Using Equivalent Fractions

1. $\frac{2}{50} = \frac{\square}{100}$ or ________%
2. $\frac{4}{25} = \frac{\square}{100}$ or ________%
3. $\frac{13}{20} =$ ________%
4. $\frac{20}{25} =$ ________%
5. $\frac{1}{10} =$ ________%
6. $\frac{1}{4} =$ ________%
7. $\frac{4}{200} =$ ________%
8. $\frac{8}{400} =$ ________%

6f Real-World Percent Problems

Solve. Show your work.

1. Joshua is making a fruit punch for a party. He needs 100 cups of fruit juice to make the fruit punch. 32% of the cups of juice are apple, 45% of the cups of juice are pineapple, and the remaining cups are orange juice. How many cups of each type of fruit juice does Joshua use?

2. There are 100 sixth-grade students in a school. 67% of these students take the bus to school, 18% walk to school. The rest of the students bike to school. How many sixth-grade students use each type of transportation to school?

3. Of the 25 students in Mr. Smith's math class, 12 like Geometry best, 7 like Algebra best, and the rest prefer Statistics. What percent of the students in the math class like each topic of mathematics best?

6g Finding Percent of a Whole Number

Example

Find 25% of 12.

Method 1:

$1\% = 0.01$

$0.01 \times 12 = 0.12$

$0.12 \times 25 = 3$

Method 2:

Express 25% as a fraction.

$25\% = \frac{25}{100}$

$\frac{25}{100} \times 12 = \frac{300}{100}$

$= 3$

Solve using method 1.

1. Find 40% of 15.

   $0.01 \times 15 =$ __________

   so __________ $\times 40 =$ __________

2. Find 72% of 800.

   $0.01 \times 800 =$ __________

   so __________ $\times 72 =$ __________

Solve using method 2.

3. Find 62% of 950.

   $62\% = \frac{\square}{100}$

   so $\frac{\square}{100} \times 950 =$ __________

4. Find 2% of 1400.

   $2\% = \frac{\square}{\square}$

   so, $\frac{\square}{\square} \times$ __________ = __________

6h Finding Percent of a Whole Number

Choose one method to solve.

1. 50% of 12 = __________

2. 4% of 60 = __________

3. 12% of 350 = __________

4. 73% of 190 = __________

Solve.

5. 2.5% of 16 = __________

6. 130% of 190 = __________

7. 45% of 1.9 = __________

8. 0.5% of 84 = __________

6i Real-World Percent Problems

In 2018, there were about 326 million people living in the United States. The table shows the blood types in the United States. Find the number of people with each blood type.

Complete the table. Use a calculator to help you.

Blood Type	Percent of the Population in the United States (in %)	Number of People in the United States (in millions)
O positive	38	
O negative	7	
A positive	34	
A negative	6	
B positive	9	
B negative	2	
AB positive	3	
AB negative	1	

6j Real-World Percent Problems

Solve. Show your work.

1. There are about 340 breeds of dogs that are recognized by the World Canine Organization. However, the American Kennel Club only recognizes 190 breeds of dogs. What percent of the breeds of dogs recognized by the World Canine Organization are recognized by the American Kennel Club? Round your answer to the nearest percent.

2. The best National Basketball Association (NBA) record in history was broken by the Golden State Warriors in 2016. They won 73 games in an 82-game season. What percent of the games did the Golden State Warriors win in 2016? Round your answer to the nearest percent.

6k Real-World Percent Problems

Connor wants to buy these three toys.

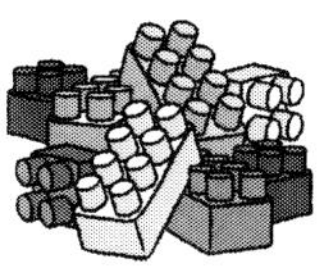

Building block set
$25

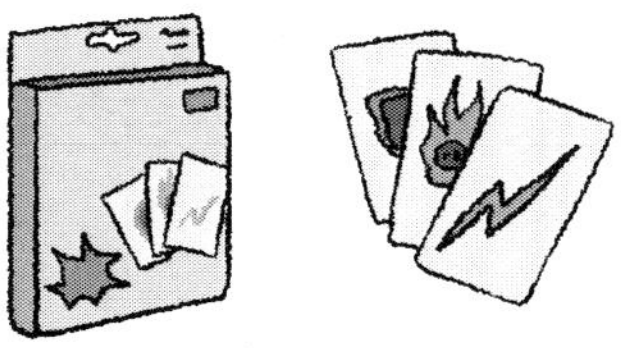

Card game
$16

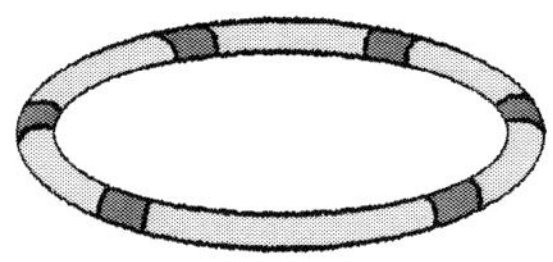

Hula hoop
$14

He has two coupons.

Coupon 1

Coupon 2

Connor wants to spend the least amount on these toys. But he can only use one coupon. Which coupon should Connor use? Show your work to justify your answer.

6l More Practice on Multiplication and Division

Solve as quickly as you can. Have a partner time you. **Time:** ______

1. $8 \times 9 =$ ______
2. $9 \times 9 =$ ______
3. $6 \times 9 =$ ______
4. $7 \times 8 =$ ______
5. $7 \times 5 =$ ______
6. $6 \times 7 =$ ______
7. $28 \div 7 =$ ______
8. $48 \div 8 =$ ______
9. $81 \div 9 =$ ______
10. $49 \div 7 =$ ______
11. $36 \div 6 =$ ______
12. $63 \div 9 =$ ______

6m Rectangles and Triangles

MATH is a rectangle.

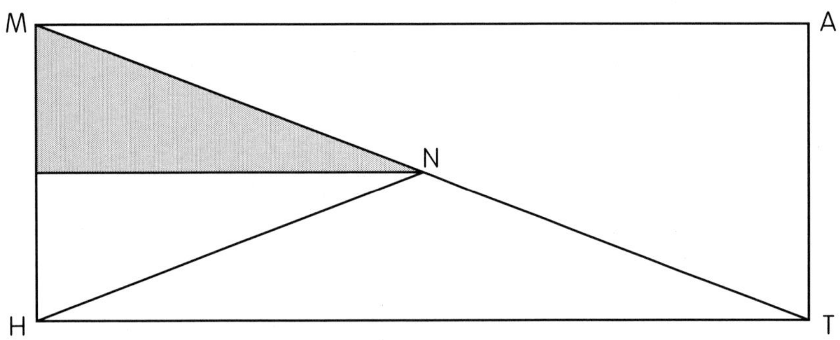

Use the clues to solve. Use a calculator to help you.

Clue 1: MT divides the rectangle in equal halves.
Clue 2: The area of the shaded triangle is 25% of the area of triangle *MHT*.
Clue 3: The area of rectangle MATH is 180 ft^2.

1. Find the area of the shaded part.

2. Was this problem challenging for you? Give a specific example of why or why not.

______

______

______

Name: ______________________ Date: ______________

Chapter 7 Fact Fluency
Algebraic Expressions

7a Real-World Addition and Subtraction Expression Problems

Greenwich Mean Time (GMT) is the clock time at the Old Royal Observatory in Greenwich, London. GMT started in 1884. All time zones around the world can be shown in GMT. It helps us tell the standardized time at any location.

Paris, France	GMT + 1 hour
Athens, Greece	GMT + 2 hours
Moscow, Russia	GMT + 3 hours
Kabul, Afghanistan	GMT + 4 hours
New Delhi, India	GMT + 5 hours
Dhaka, Bangladesh	GMT + 6 hours

Bangkok, Thailand	GMT + 7 hours
Singapore	GMT + 8 hours
Tokyo, Japan	GMT + 9 hours
Honolulu, United States	GMT – 10 hours
Denver, United States	GMT – 7 hours
New York, United States	GMT – 5 hours

Use the information in the table to answer each question. Use the variable, *g*, to represent GMT.

1. Write an expression to represent the time in Singapore in terms of g. ____________
2. Write an expression to represent the time in Denver in terms of g. ____________
3. What time is it in Tokyo, Japan, if it is 5:00 pm in Greenwich, London, on Feb 2nd, 2019? ____________
4. What time is it in Denver when it is 11:00 pm in New Delhi, India? ____________

7b Multiplication Expressions

Evaluate each expression when $x = 6$, $y = 7$, $z = 8$, and $r = 9$.

1. $3x =$ $3y =$ $3z =$ $3r =$
2. $4x =$ $4z =$ $4x + 4z =$ $4z + 4r =$
3. $6x + 3y =$
4. $5z + 9r =$
5. $2y - 2x =$

Use a calculator to evaluate.

6. $8xyz + 5ryz + 3rxy =$

7c More Practice on Single-Digit Division

Solve as quickly as you can. Have a partner time you. **Time:** ____________

1. $42 \div 7 =$ ____________
2. $42 \div 6 =$ ____________
3. $48 \div 6 =$ ____________
4. $32 \div 8 =$ ____________
5. $24 \div 3 =$ ____________
6. $81 \div 9 =$ ____________
7. $16 \div 8 =$ ____________
8. $24 \div 6 =$ ____________
9. $100 \div 10 =$ ____________

10. **Each brick is the product of the two bricks below it. Fill in the missing numbers.**

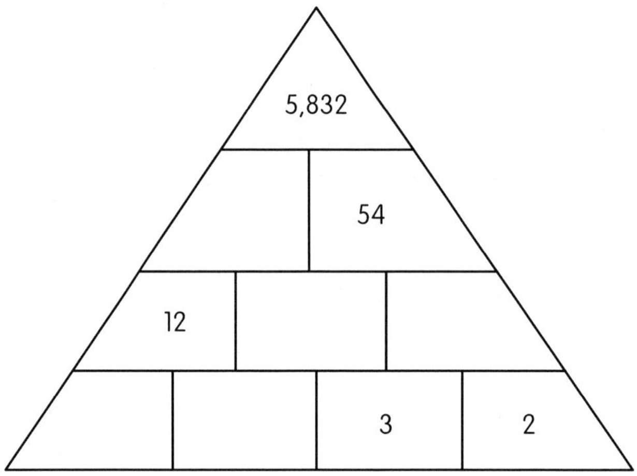

7d Division Expressions

Evaluate each expression given the value of the variables.

1. $\frac{27}{a} =$ ____________ when $a = 3$
2. $32 \div x =$ ____________ when $x = 4$
3. $w \div 3 =$ ____________ when $w = 27$
4. $\frac{n}{10} =$ ____________ when $n = 50$
5. $81 \div n =$ ____________ when $n = 9$
6. $\frac{48}{p} =$ ____________ when $p = 6$

7e Mixed Expressions

Use the clues to help you find the variables.

1.
Clue 1: a is greater than b.
Clue 2: b is $\frac{1}{3}$ of c.
Clue 3: $\frac{35}{a} = 7$
Clue 4: $a + 4 = c$

a = ______________

b = ______________

c = ______________

2.
Clue 1: $7r = 8r - 5$
Clue 2: $r = p + 2$
Clue 3: $9 \div 3 = p$
Clue 4: $p = 5 - q$

r = ______________

p = ______________

q = ______________

3.
Clue 1: $2x - 2 = y$
Clue 2: $x + 1 = y$

x = ______________

y = ______________

7f Mixed Multiplication and Division

1. List all of the multiplication facts that have a product of 24.

Example
3 × 8

2. What was your strategy?

____

____

3. List all of the division facts within 100 that give a quotient of 3.

Example
24 ÷ 8

4. What was your strategy? Did you notice anything about the division facts? Explain your observation.

____

____

____

7g Real-World Multiplication Expression Problems

For each story, write the algebraic expression and solve it.

1. Michael wants to buy an airline ticket to New York. It is twice as much to buy a non-stop ticket than to buy a ticket that makes a connection in Chicago. The cost of the connecting ticket to Chicago is x dollars.

   a Write an expression for the non-stop ticket in terms of x. ____________

   b If the connecting ticket to Chicago costs \$200, how much is the non-stop ticket? \$____________

2. Hannah is moving to a new apartment. Her new apartment is 4 times the walking distance in meters to her school than her old apartment. The walking distance from her old apartment to her school is d meters.

   a Write an expression for the walking distance from Hannah's new apartment to her school in terms of d. ____________ m

   b Hannah used to walk 150 meters from her old apartment to school. How far does she need to walk now? ____________ m

7h Real-World Division Expression Problems

For each story, write the algebraic expression and solve it.

1. Dylan and Eric were the lead scorers in a basketball game. Dylan scored j points in the second period of the game. Eric scored $\frac{1}{2}$ as many points as Dylan in the same period of the game.

   a Write an expression for Eric's score in terms of j. ____________

   b If Dylan scored 18 points in the second period, how many points did Eric score? ____________

2. Mariah was raising money for an animal shelter. She raised $\frac{1}{5}$ as much money on Monday than she did on Tuesday. The amount of money she raised on Tuesday was t dollars.

   a Write an expression for the amount of money Mariah raised on Monday in terms of t. \$____________

   b If Mariah raised \$125 on Tuesday, how much money did she raise on Monday? \$____________

7i More Practice on Single-Digit Multiplication

Solve.

1. ○ × □ = 63
   ◇ × ◇ = □
   ◇ × ○ = ____________

2. ✶ + ✶ + ✶ = 27
   ✶ × ■ = 36
   ■ = ____________

3. ⊙ × ⊙ = 49
   ⊙ × ____________ = ✪
   ✪ + 2 = 58

7j Real-World Multiplication and Division Expression Problems

Anthony is building a tree house in his backyard. He draws a sketch of the tree house.

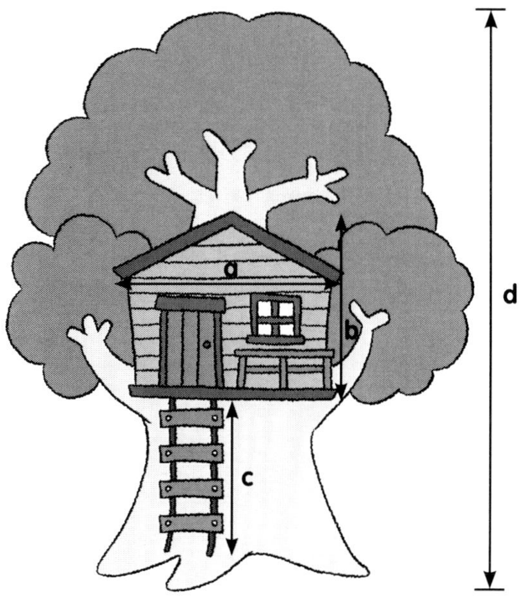

To plan for the dimensions of the actual tree house, help Anthony write an expression for each of the following:

1. The width of the actual tree house must be 4 times the width of the sketch. ____________ feet
2. The height of the actual tree house must be 5 times the height of the sketch. ____________ feet
3. The ladder of the actual tree house must be $\frac{1}{8}$ of the height of the tree. ____________ feet
4. The height of the entire tree house must be $\frac{1}{4}$ of the height of the tree. ____________ feet

If the tree is 80 feet tall,

5. how tall should the entire tree house be? ____________ feet
6. how tall should the ladder be? ____________ feet

7k Practice on Fractions

Add. Express your answer in simplest form.

1. $\frac{1}{2} + \frac{1}{2} =$ ______

2. $\frac{3}{4} + \frac{1}{4} =$ ______

3. $\frac{2}{3} + \frac{1}{3} =$ ______

4. $\frac{8}{10} + \frac{1}{10} =$ ______

5. $\frac{2}{8} + \frac{3}{8} =$ ______

6. $\frac{1}{2} + \frac{1}{4} =$ ______

7. $\frac{2}{3} + \frac{1}{6} =$ ______

8. $\frac{2}{5} + \frac{3}{10} =$ ______

9. $\frac{2}{3} + \frac{4}{6} =$ ______

10. $\frac{1}{2} + \frac{1}{3} =$ ______

11. $\frac{2}{3} + \frac{1}{4} =$ ______

12. $\frac{3}{4} + \frac{4}{5} =$ ______

7l Practice on Decimals

Solve.

1. 1.2 + 1.4 = ______

2. 2.4 + 3.2 = ______

3. 0.45 – 0.32 = ______

4. 2.7 + 1.3 = ______

5. 7.6 + 1.3 = ______

6. 3.4 + 5.7 = ______

Rewrite each problem vertically. Then, solve.

7. 9.01 – 6.2 = ______

8. 0.08 + 0.4 = ______

9. 0.045 – 0.007 = ______

Rewrite:

$$\begin{array}{r} 9.01 \\ -\ 6.2 \\ \hline \end{array}$$

Rewrite:

Rewrite:

7m Real-World Fraction Expression Problems

Empire Middle School wants some new classes for the art department. They asked all the sixth-grade students to suggest the classes they are interested in.

Class Title	Number of Students Interested in the Class
Pottery	a
Drawing	r
Photography	t
Painting	s

Use the table above and write each expression.

1. One quarter of the students who are interested in pottery will take the class. ____________
2. One half of the students interested in photography will be enrolled in the class. ____________
3. Two-thirds of the students interested in the painting class are girls. ____________
4. If there are 198 students interested in the painting, how many of them are girls? ____________
5. The students interested in drawing are $\frac{1}{3}$ of the total number of students. ____________
6. There are 369 students in all. How many of the students are interested in the drawing class? ____________

7n Real-World Decimal Expression Problems

Samuel is shopping at a bookstore.

$0.45

$1.20

$2.30

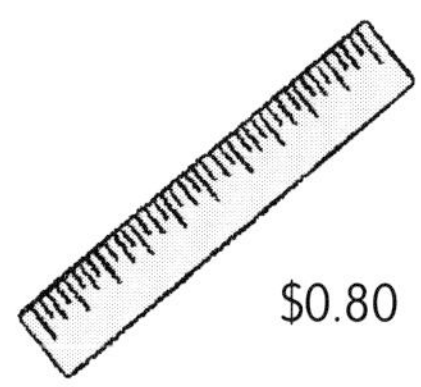

$0.80

1. Samuel wants to buy p number of pencils. Write an expression for the total cost of pencils in terms of p. ____________
2. Samuel wants to buy n number of pens. Write an expression for the total cost of pens in terms of n. ____________

3. Samuel wants to buy *b* number of notebooks. Write an expression for the cost of each notebook in terms of *b*. ______

4. Samuel wants to buy *r* number of rulers. Write an expression for the cost of each ruler in terms of *r*. ______

5. Write an expression for the total cost of *r* rulers and *b* notebooks. ______

6. If $p = 4$ and $n = 3$, how much would John spend on pencils and pens? ______

7. If Samuel spends between $9 and $10, what is one possible combination of items that he could buy? Show your work. ______

7o Algebraic Expressions

In real-life situations, we can write an algebraic expression in which some of the information is unknown.

Example

Caleb drives at an average speed of 55 mph to and from a shopping mall. His sister drives at an average speed of (x + 55) mph for the same distance.

Name three additional examples in which you might write an algebraic expression.

1. ______

______

______

2. ______

______

______

3. ______

______

______

Name: ______________________ Date: ______________

Chapter 8 Fact Fluency
Equations and Inequalities

8a Writing Numerical Equations

Complete the sentence to make each statement true.

1. **Sum** is the solution to an ____________ problem.
2. **Difference** is the solution to a ____________ problem.
3. **Product** is the solution to a ____________ problem.
4. **Quotient** is the solution to a ____________ problem.
5. Two other ways to say **equal** are ____________ and ____________.

Write an equation to represent each situation.

Example
100 more than 52 is the same as 90 added to 62.
$52 + 100 = 62 + 90$

6. 36 minus 18 is the same as 9 multiplied by 2. ____________
7. 2 plus 2 plus 2 is equivalent to 19 minus 13. ____________
8. 4 times 7 is equivalent to 16 more than 4 added to 8. ____________
9. The difference between 900 and 750 is the same as the sum of 100 and 50. ____________
10. The product of 4.5 and 2 is equal to the quotient of 18 and 2. ____________
11. The sum of $\frac{1}{2}$ and $\frac{3}{4}$ is equivalent to the product of $\frac{1}{4}$ and 5. ____________

8b Solving Numerical Equations

Solve each equation. Is the equation true? Circle True or False. Then, justify your answer.

1. $8 + 2 - 5 = 15 - 10$ True / False How do you know? ______
2. $19 \times 3 = 42 - 5$ True / False How do you know? ______
3. $7 - 3.5 = 9 - 6.55$ True / False How do you know? ______
4. $2 \div 4 = \frac{1}{2} + \frac{1}{2}$ True / False How do you know? ______
5. $3.4 \div 1.2 = 1.2 + 1.2 - 1.2 - 1.2$ True / False How do you know? ______

8c Writing Algebraic Expressions

For each question, define the variable. Then, write the algebraic expressions using the given variable.

1. Zara is t inches tall. $t =$ ______

   Jacob is 4 inches taller than Zara. ______

   Madison is $3\frac{1}{2}$ inches shorter than Zara. ______

2. It is d degrees in San Francisco. $d =$ ______

   It is 9°F warmer in San Mateo than in San Francisco. ______

   It is 20°F colder in St. Louis than in San Francisco. ______

3. A tomato plant grows x centimeters each day. $x =$ ______

   A basil plant grows twice as quickly as a tomato plant. ______

   A bell pepper grows $\frac{1}{3}$ as quickly as a tomato plant. ______

4. Ana runs m miles in 15 minutes. $m =$ ______

   Jade runs 1 mile more than Ana in 15 minutes. ______

   Zoe runs 0.8 miles more than Jade in 15 minutes. ______

8d Simplifying Algebraic Expressions

A package has *t* pieces of rabbit treats.

1. Define the variable. $t =$ ______________

2. Laura has several rabbits. She wants to find out the maximum number of treats each rabbit can receive equally for a week in the following situations. The rabbits cannot receive a part of a treat.

Complete the table.

Number of packages	Number of rabbits	Number of treats each rabbit receives	
		when $t = 10$	When $t = 15$
3	3		
5	3		
1	2		
4	2		
	2	25	
4			15

8e Solving Algebraic Expressions

Solve each equation. The first one has been done for you.

$5 = y + 4$	$12 \div p = 6$	$n = 3 \times 3$	$8 \div w = 2$	$5x = 15$	$p + 5 = 10$	$m + 3 = 9$	$5 = y + 4$	$r - 4 = 4$
1	____	____	____	____	____	____	____	____

Then, use the chart below to break the code. Use your answers in order.

1	2	3	4	5	6	7	8	9
I	S	V	L	E	D	P	T	O

I ____ ____ ____ ____ ____ ____ ____ ____!

8f Writing Algebraic Expressions

Example

Expression 1: $x + 3$ Expression 2: $2x - 1$

I can write an equation to make Expression 1 equal to Expression 2.

Equation: $x + 3 = 2x - 1$

An equation shows that two expressions are equal.

For each story, write an algebraic equation.

1. Lucas buys 3 packages of x pencils. Jaden buys 2 packages of x pencils and 6 more pencils. They pay the same price.

2. Taylor's cat eats 2 containers of m pounds of cat food each month. David's cat eats 4 containers of m pounds of cat food each month and has 6 pounds left over. Both cats eat the same amount of cat food in each month.

8g Writing an Algebraic Linear Equation from a Table

The table below shows the relationship between the number of bottles of lemonade and the number of cups of lemonade.

1. Complete the table.

Bottles of Lemonade (*b*)	1	2	3	4	5	8
Cups of Lemonade (*c*)	8	16	24	32		

2. Write an equation to show the relationship between the bottles of lemonade and the cups of lemonade.

____

The table below shows the relationship between the number of correct answers and the final score Emma got in a game.

3. Complete the table.

Number of Correct Answers (*n*)	1	2	3	4	10	25
Emma's Final Score (*p*)	4	8	12	16		

4. Write an equation to show the relationship between the number of correct answers Emma got and her final score.

____

8h Real-World Algebraic Linear Equation Problems

Alex and James bought new wallets. James spent x dollars on his wallet. Alex spent $7 more than James on his wallet.

1. If the amount of money Alex spent on his wallet is y dollars, express y in terms of x. __________

2. If James spent $30 on his wallet, how much did Alex spend on his wallet? __________

3. If Alex spent $15 on his wallet, how much did James spend on his wallet? __________

4. If the total amount of money James and Alex spent on their wallets was t dollars, express t in terms of x. __________

5. If James and Alex spent $97 in all, how much did each of them spend? __________

8i Writing Inequalities

For each question, write an inequality.

1. 5 is less than 10 __________

2. 17 is more than 5 __________

For each question, write an inequality comparing the ages.

3. Isaac is 27 years old. Sean is 45 years old. __________

4. Kayla is 72 years old. Alyssa is 67 years old. __________

Represent each inequality on a number line.

5. All numbers less than or equal to 4.

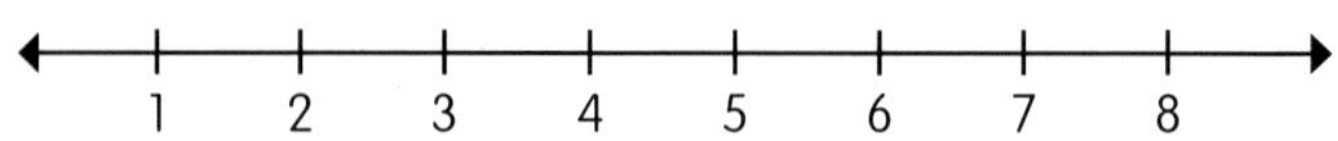

6. All numbers greater than $\frac{1}{2}$.

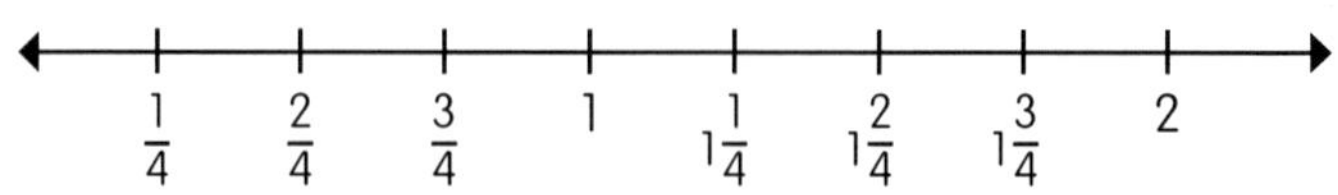

8j Writing Algebraic Inequalities

An algebraic inequality is the method of writing an inequality statement where we use a variable to represent one of the quantities.

Example

Represent $x < 7$ on a number line.

The inequality $x < 7$ is true for any values less than 7.

←—○ represents less than.

○—→ represents more than.

←—● represents less than or equal to.

●—→ represents more than or equal to.

1. Amy buys some flowers for her grandmother. The bunch that she chooses has at least 8 flowers. Write an inequality to represent the bunch of flowers Amy buys for her grandmother. Represent the inequality on a number line.

2. Mr. Young has $10.25 for lunch. Write an inequality to represent the amount of money he can spend on his lunch. Represent the inequality on a number line.

8k Writing Algebraic Inequalities

1. Match each phrase to its inequality.

at least 6 •	• $x \geq 6$
more than 6 •	• $3 \leq x \leq 6$
at most 6 •	• $x \leq 6$
less than 6 •	• $x > 6$
between 3 and 6 •	• $x < 6$

2. Write a story for any inequality above.

____

____

____

8l Writing Algebraic Inequalities

A sixth-grade class is studying animal behavior. They make observations about the animals in the zoo. Define the variable. Then, write the algebraic equation or inequality for each observation.

Example

There are at least 3 tigers in the tiger enclosure.

t = number of tigers

$t \geq 3$

1. There are at least 25 naked mole rats in the maze.

2. There are 3,500 animals in the zoo.

3. The zoo houses more than 700,000 exotic plants.

4. Honey bees are no more than 0.6 inches long.

5. African dwarf crocodiles can grow up to 5 feet in length.

8m Solving Algebraic Inequalities

You can solve an **algebraic inequality** by graphing. In this method, all of the possible solutions are shown on a number line. Remember that a shaded circle on a number line includes the number below the circle as a solution while an empty circle does not.

Graph the inequality on a number line to show the possible solutions. Then, test a solution.

Example

$x \leq 4$

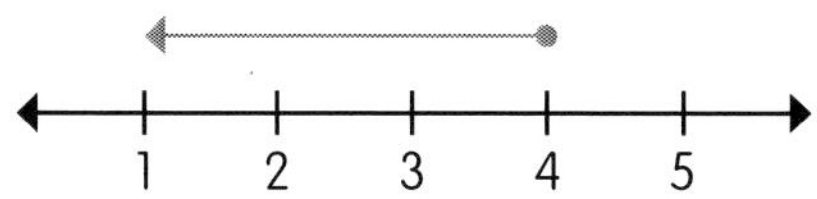

When $x = 2$,

$2 \leq 4$

The inequality, $x \leq 4$, is true.

1. $t \leq 3$

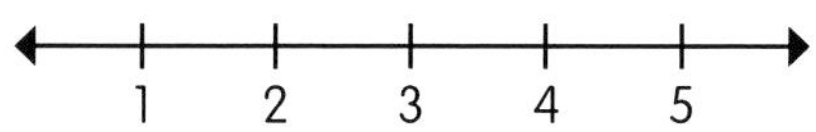

2. $x > -2$

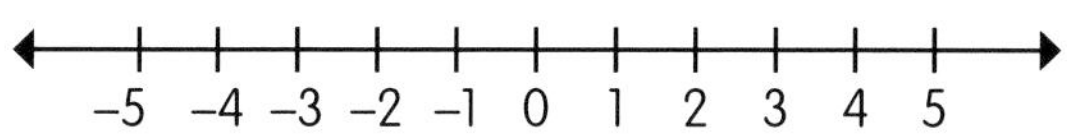

3. $n < 4.5$

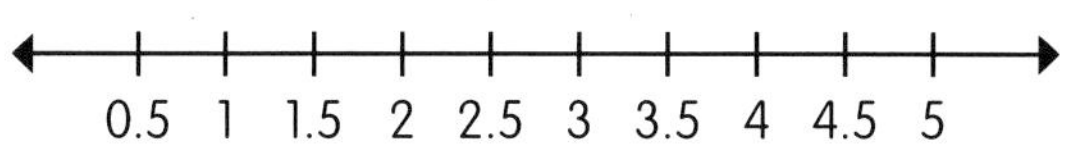

4. $p \geq -1.5$

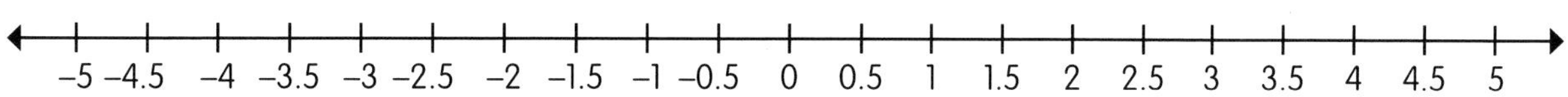

8n Real-World Algebraic Inequality Problems

Mr. Parker is organizing his students to deliver fruit baskets to a local hospital.

He needs to have enough vans for 35 students. Each van can hold a maximum of 12 students.

1. Write an inequality to represent the number of vans Mr. Parker will need for his students.

2. Does the inequality in 1 have more than one solution? Justify your answer.

3. Would a graph of this solution be reasonable? Explain.

8o Expressions, Equations, and Inequalities

Define each term in your own words. Then, provide an example.

1. Numerical expression

   Definition: __________

   Example:

2. Algebraic expression

   Definition: __________

Example:

3. Algebraic equation

Definition: ____

____

____

Example:

4. Numerical inequality

Definition: ____

____

____

Example:

5. Algebraic inequality

Definition: ____

____

____

Example:

BLANK

Name: ______________________ Date: ______________

Chapter 9

Fact Fluency
The Coordinate Plane

9a Integers on a Number Line

1 **Draw a vertical number line to represent each integer.**

a −5 b 5 c −2 d 0 e 3

2 **Draw a horizontal number line to represent each integer.**

a 1 b 0 c −4 d −1 e 2

9b Using a Coordinate Plane

You can put the vertical and horizontal number lines together to create a **coordinate plane.**

The horizontal number line is called the ***x*-axis**. The vertical number line is called the ***y*-axis**.

You can find a location of a point on the coordinate plane using an ordered pair, (***x***, ***y***).

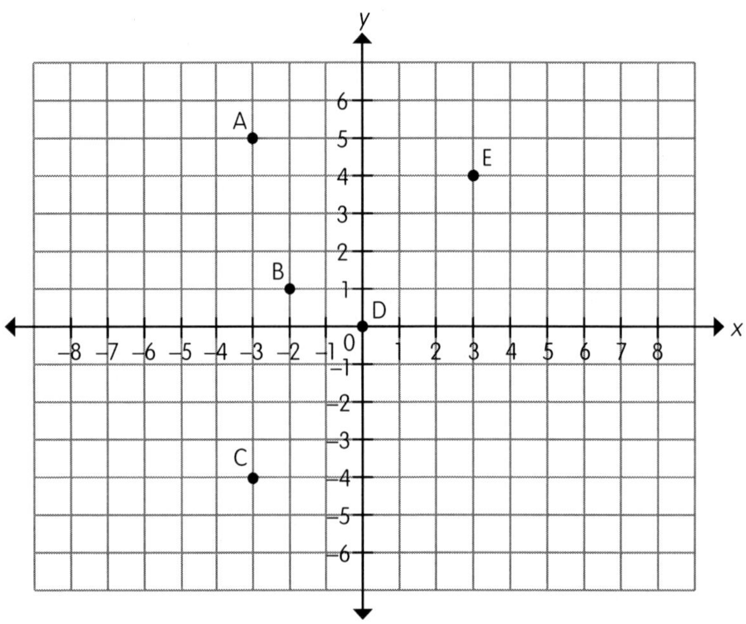

Match each point on the above coordinate plane with the given coordinates.

Example

(–3, 5) A

1. (0, 0) ____________
2. (3, 4) ____________
3. (–2, 1) ____________
4. (–3, –4) ____________

9c Plotting Points from a Table

Use each set of ordered pairs in the table to plot the points on the coordinate plane. Draw a line segment to connect them.

x	–1	–2	–3	0	1	2	3
y	1	2	3	0	–1	–2	–3

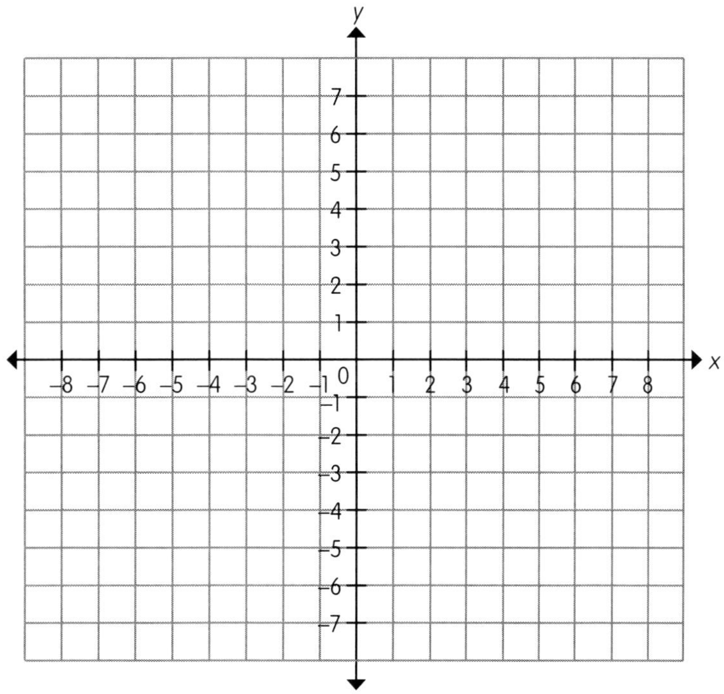

9d Using Absolute Value to Find Distance

Example

Find the length of the line segment, $\overline{AB}$.

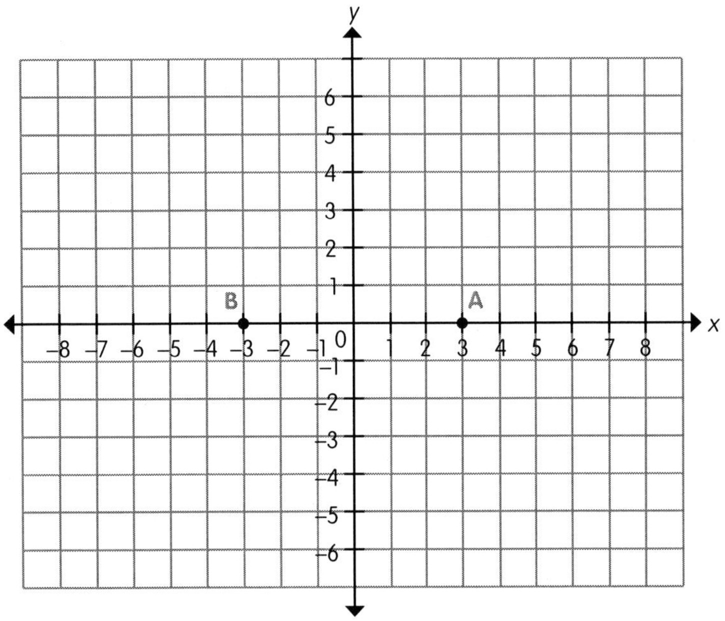

The coordinates are A (3, 0) and B (–3, 0).

The distance from 3 to –3 can be counted in this way:

$$\begin{aligned} AB &= AO + OB \\ &= 3 + |-3| \\ &= 3 + 3 \\ &= 6 \end{aligned}$$

The length of $\overline{AB}$ is 6 units.

You can determine the length of a horizontal or vertical line in the coordinate plane using the absolute value of the end points of the line.

Find the length of each line segment.

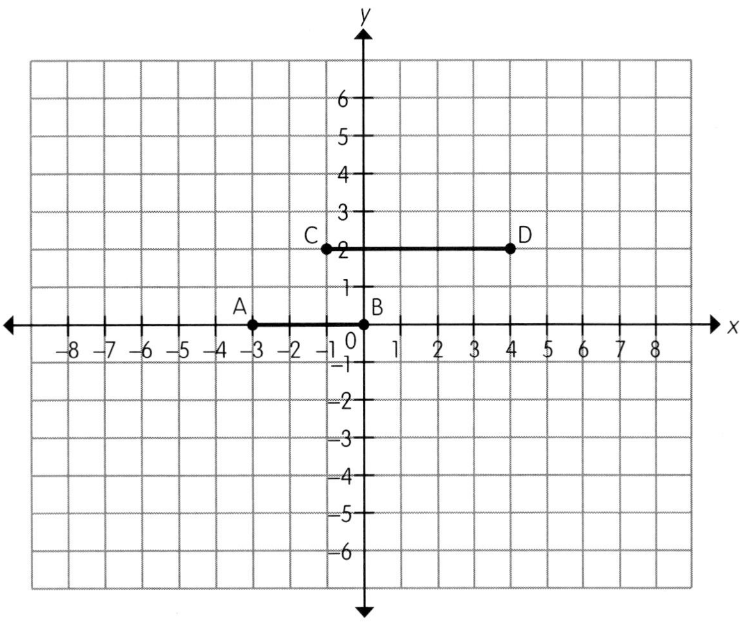

1. $\overline{AB}$ is ________ units.

2. $\overline{CD}$ is ________ units.

9e Finding Perimeter of Polygons

The perimeter of a shape is the total distance around it. Find the perimeter of each polygon.

1. 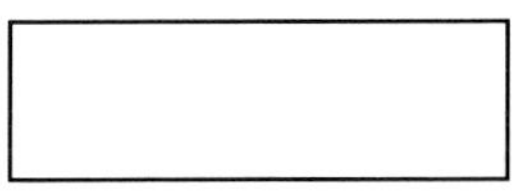

Length = 2 ft

Width = 1.5 ft

Perimeter = ________

2. 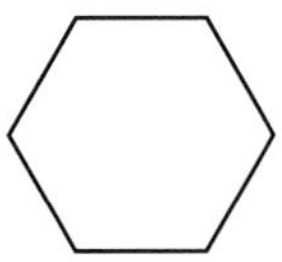

Side = $5\frac{1}{4}$ cm

Perimeter = ________

3. 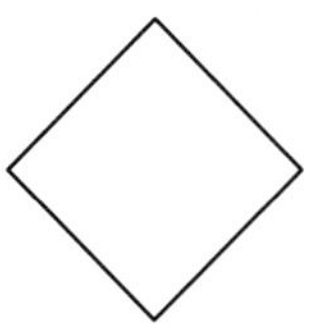

Side = 3.02 in.

Perimeter = ________

4 A rectangle and an equilateral triangle are combined to make this new shape. Find the perimeter of the new shape. Show your work.

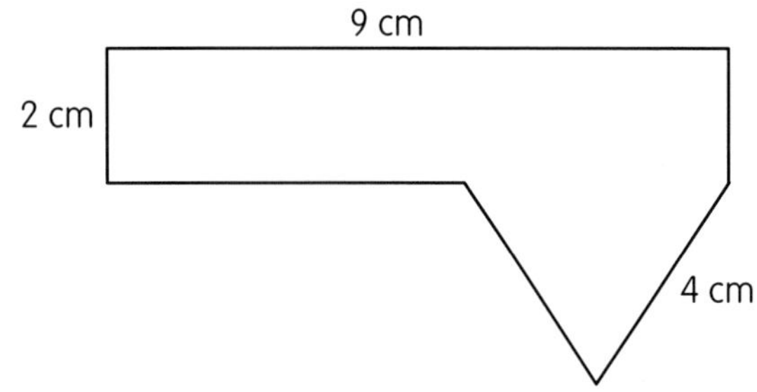

9f Finding Perimeter of Polygons on Coordinate Planes

A rectangle ABCD is shown in the diagram below.

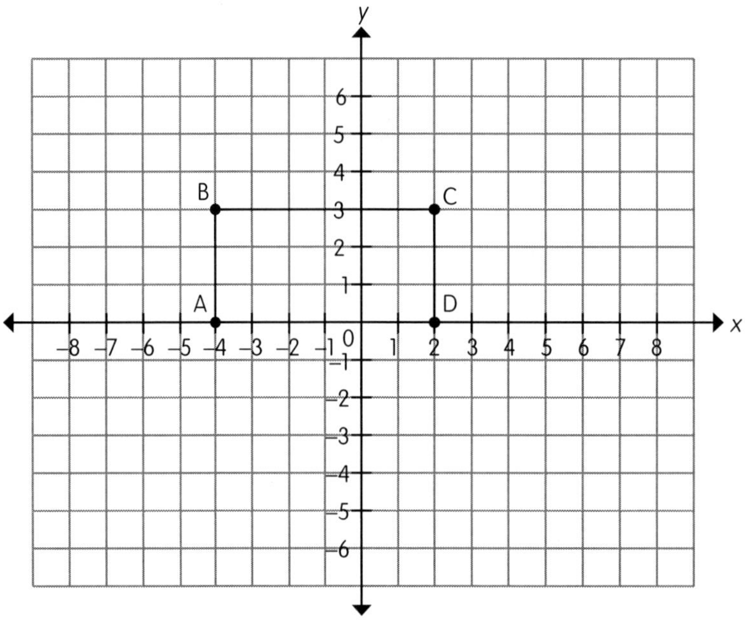

Find the perimeter of ABCD by finding the length of each line segment.

AB = ___________ units BC = ___________ units CD = ___________ units DA = ___________ units

Perimeter of rectangle ABCD =

9g Real-World Perimeter of Polygon Problems

Mr. Martin is building a terrarium. His rectangular terrarium has a perimeter of 64 inches. Help Mr. Martin plot his terrarium on the coordinate plane.

1. Choose the coordinates of points A, B, C, and D of his terrarium.

   A: (____________, ____________)

   B: (____________, ____________)

   C: (____________, ____________)

   D: (____________, ____________)

2. Plot all coordinates of his terrarium on the coordinate plane.

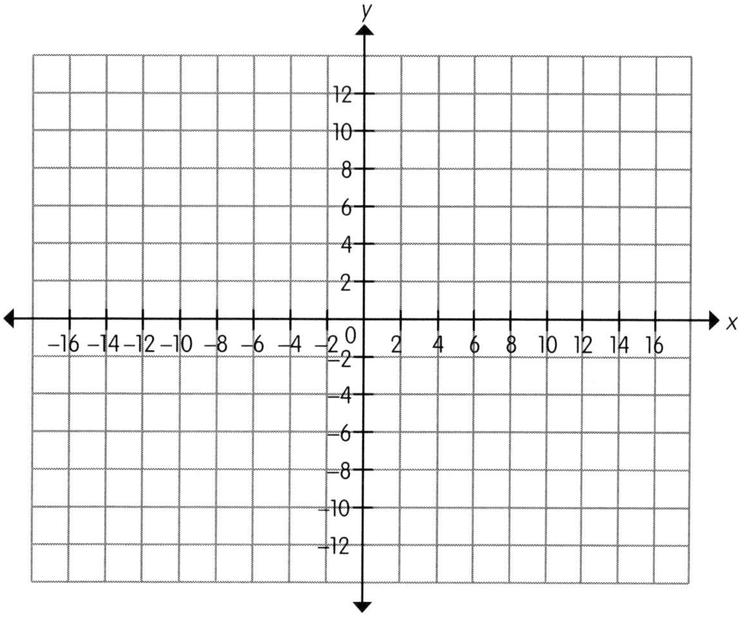

3. How do you know the perimeter is 64 inches on the coordinate plane? Explain your thinking.

____

____

____

9h The Coordinate Plane

1. How is the coordinate plane similar to a number line?

2. How is the coordinate plane different from a number line?

3. When might a number line be the best representation of data?

4. Use an example to explain when a coordinate plane would be a better representation than a number line.

Name: ______________________ Date: ____________

Chapter 10 Fact Fluency
Area of Polygons

10a More Practice on Multiplying Fractions

Solve.

1. $2 \times \frac{1}{2} =$ ________
2. $\frac{3}{4} \times 20 =$ ________
3. $3 \times \frac{1}{4} =$ ________
4. $\frac{1}{5} \times 8 =$ ________
5. $\frac{2}{5} \times 24 =$ ________
6. $6 \times \frac{2}{7} =$ ________
7. $\frac{1}{3} \times \frac{1}{4} =$ ________
8. $\frac{2}{3} \times \frac{1}{4} =$ ________
9. $\frac{2}{3} \times \frac{2}{4} =$ ________
10. $\frac{1}{2} \times 1\frac{1}{2} =$ ________
11. $\frac{2}{3} \times 1\frac{1}{3} =$ ________
12. $\frac{3}{5} \times 2\frac{3}{4} =$ ________

10b More Practice on Multiplying Decimals

Write each decimal as a fraction.

1. $0.3 = \frac{3}{\square}$
2. $0.06 = \frac{6}{\square}$
3. $2.35 = \frac{\square}{100}$

Write each decimal as a fraction and multiply.

4. $0.6 \times 0.8 = \frac{6}{10} \times \frac{8}{10}$

   = ________

5. $0.04 \times 0.3 = \frac{4}{100} \times \frac{\square}{\square}$

   = ________

Multiply mentally.

6. $2 \times 2.5 =$ ________
7. $4 \times 0.5 =$ ________
8. $0.25 \times 6 =$ ________

Multiply.

9. $0.8 \times 0.2 =$ ________
10. $0.01 \times 0.4 =$ ________
11. $3.5 \times 2.1 =$ ________

10c Finding Area of Quadrilaterals

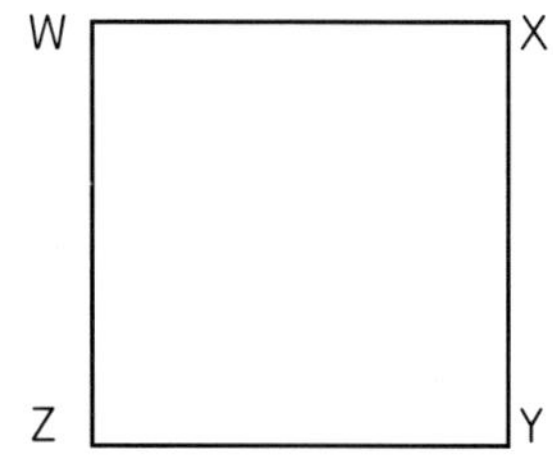

1. Find the area of rectangle ABCD when

   a. its length is 3 in. and its width is 5 in.

   Area = ____________ in^2

   b. its length is 6 in. and its width is 10 in.

   Area = ____________ in^2

2. Compare the two areas you found in 1. What do you notice?

   ____

   ____

   ____

3. Find the area of square WXYZ when

   a. its side is 3 in.

   Area = ____________ in^2

   b. its side is $1\frac{1}{2}$ in.

   Area = ____________ in^2

4. Compare the two areas you found in 3. What do you notice?

   ____

   ____

   ____

10d Finding Area of Triangles

Example

You can find the area of a triangle using the area of a rectangle or a square.

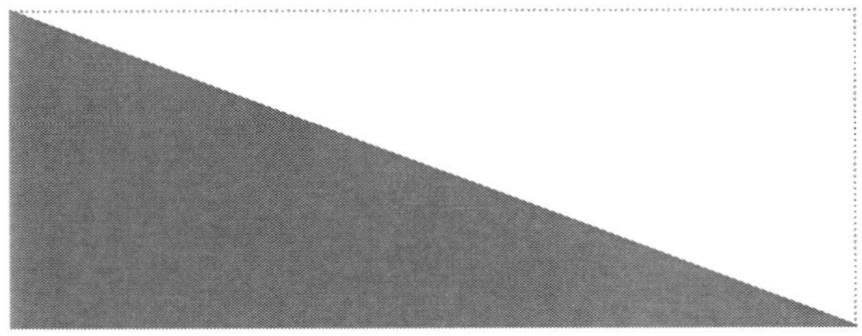

Half of a rectangle is a triangle.

So, the area of a triangle is half the area of a rectangle.

Area of triangle = $\frac{1}{2}$ × length × width

ABCD is a rectangle. Find the area of triangle BCD.

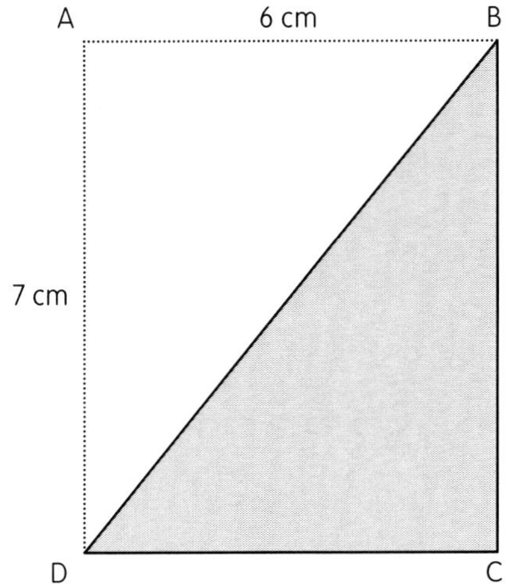

Length AD = __________ cm

Width AB = __________ cm

Area of rectangle ABCD =

Area of triangle BCD =

10e Finding Perimeter of Polygons

Find the area of each triangle.

1.

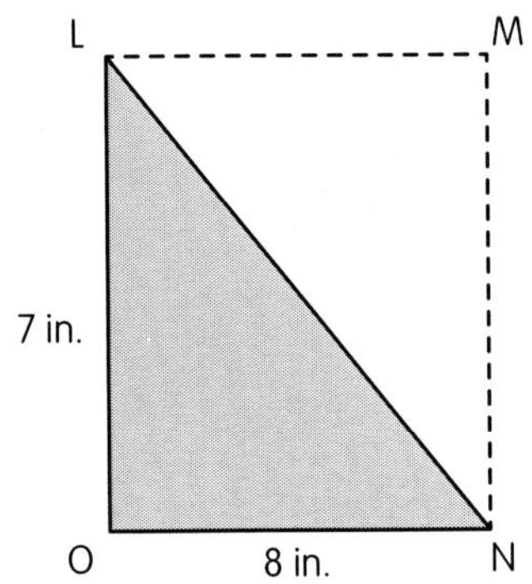

Area of rectangle LMNO =

Area of triangle LNO =

2.

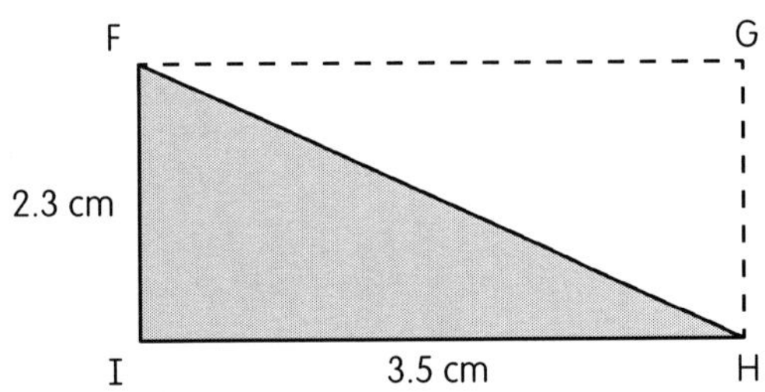

Area of rectangle FGHI =

Area of triangle FHI =

Find the area of the triangle given the base and height.

3. Base = 10 ft   Height = 6 ft   Area = ________ ft^2

4. Base = $\frac{1}{2}$ yd   Height = $\frac{3}{4}$ yd   Area = ________ yd^2

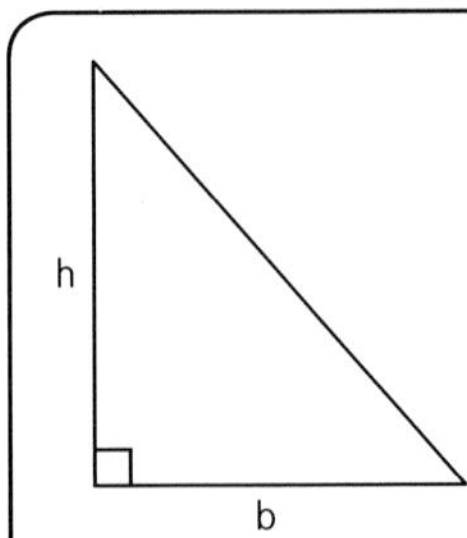

Area of triangle = $\frac{1}{2} \times b \times h$

10f Finding Area of Other Figures

Example

Find the area of the trapezoid.

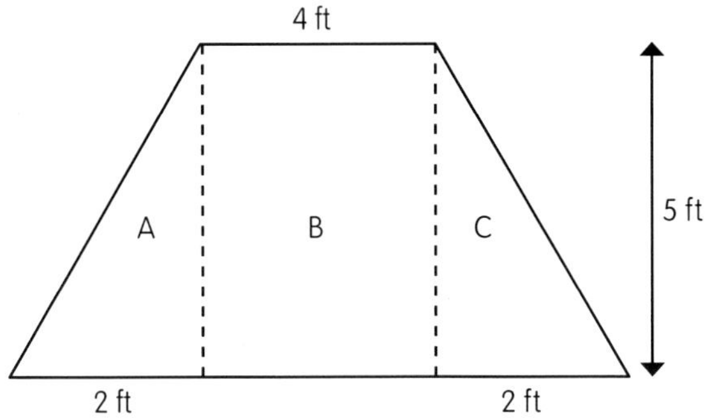

Area of triangle A $= \frac{1}{2} \times 2 \times 5$

$= 5 \text{ ft}^2$

Area of rectangle B $= 4 \times 5$

$= 20 \text{ ft}^2$

Area of triangle C = Area of triangle A

$= 5 \text{ ft}^2$

Area of trapezoid $= 5 + 20 + 5$

$= 30 \text{ ft}^2$

You can also use areas of triangles and rectangles to find the areas of trapezoids.

Find the area of the trapezoid.

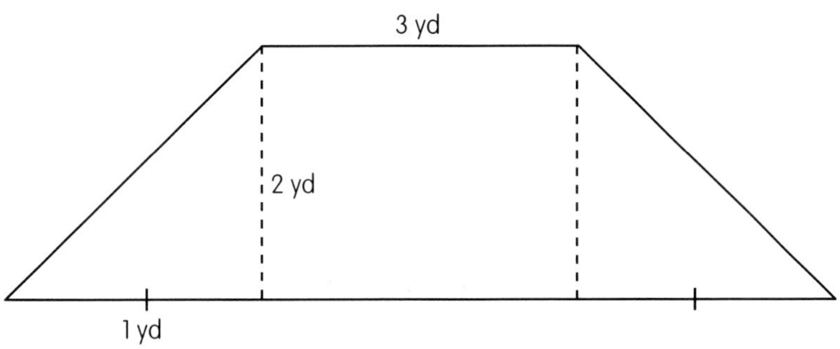

10g Finding Area of Other Figures

Find the area of each figure.

1

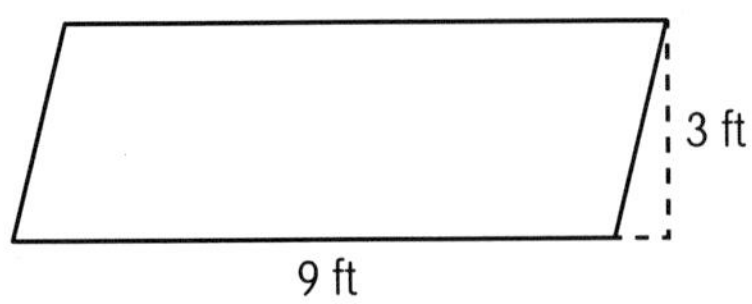

2

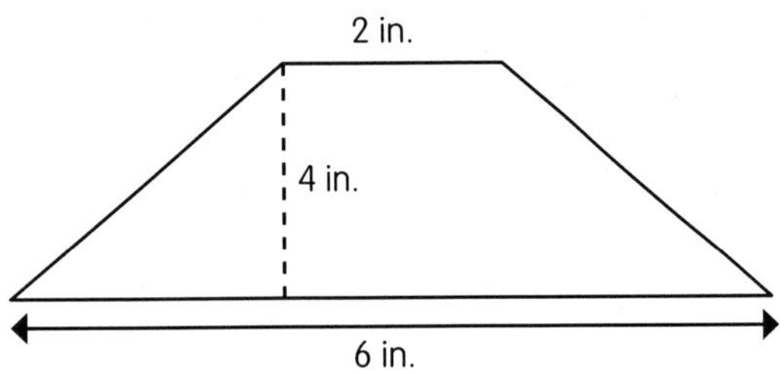

10h Finding Area of Other Figures

Find the area of each figure.

3

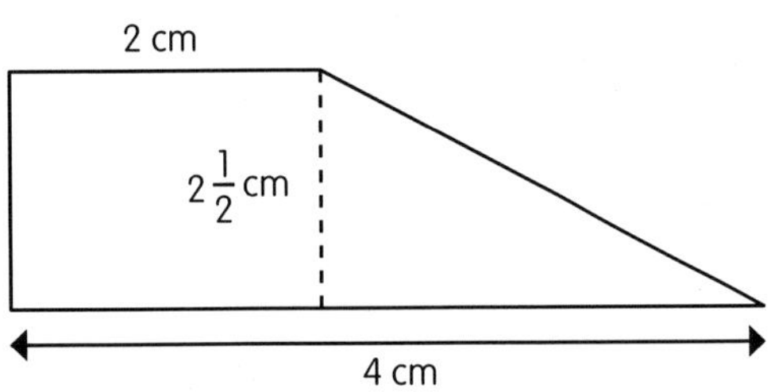

4

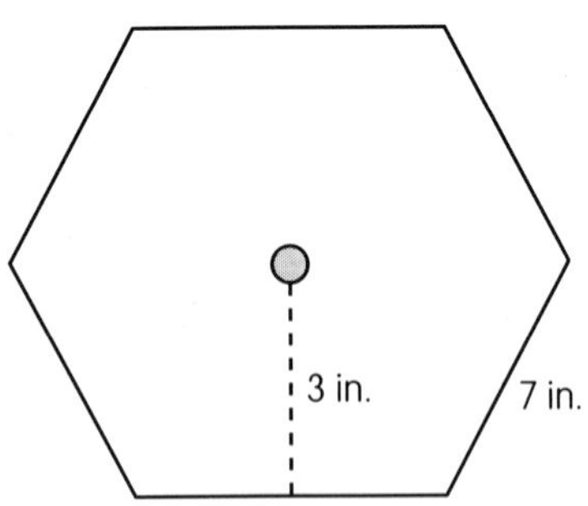

10i Real-World Area of Polygon Problems

Solve. Show your work.

1. Luke is designing a popcorn box as a prop for the school play. He wants to cover the front of the box in gold foil and then paint the remaining sides. Looking at the front view of the box, decide how much area he will need to cover in gold foil.

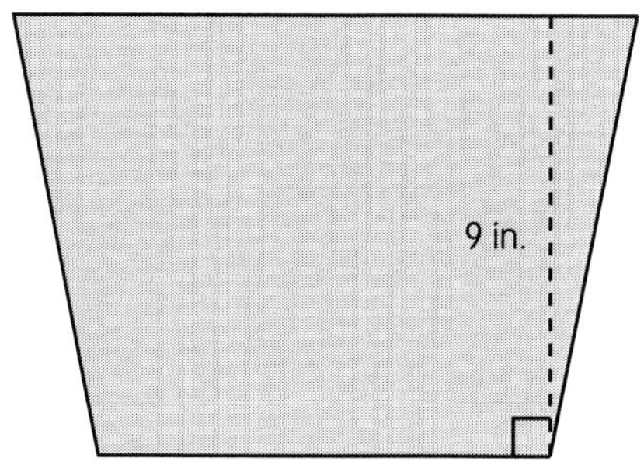

2. If the foil costs $0.44 per square inches, how much does Luke pay to cover the front of the box?

10j Finding Area of Polygons

Sketch each polygon in the table. Then, write the formula for its area.

1

Polygon	Sketch	Formula to find area
Rectangle		
Triangle		
Parallelogram		
Trapezoid		

2 Describe one pattern you notice in studying the area of the polygons.

____

____

____

3 Sketch a regular pentagon.

4 What would be an easy way to find the area of a polygon with 5 equal sides? Explain your thinking.

____

____

____

Name: ______________________ Date: ____________

Chapter 11

Fact Fluency

Surface Area and Volume of Solids

11a Order of Operations

Solve.

1. $3 + 5 - 2 \times 3 =$ ________
2. $3 \times 4 + 2 \div 2 =$ ________
3. $(4 + 2) \times 3 - 6 =$ ________
4. $5 \times 2 + 3 \times 4 =$ ________
5. $45 \div 9 \times (3 + 7) =$ ________
6. $2^2 \times 9 \div 3 - 3 =$ ________

Fill in the correct symbols (+, –, ×, or ÷) to make each equation true.

7. 4 ◯ 3 ◯ 8 ◯ 4 = 16
8. 6 ◯ 2 ◯ 4 ◯ 2 = 10

Add parentheses ( ) to make each equation true.

9. $4 \times 3 + 2 - 6 = 14$
10. $3 \times 3 \times 3 + 1 = 36$

11b Commutative and Associative Properties of Multiplication

Commutative property comes from the Latin prefix *com-* which means "with" and the root *-mut* which means "change".

Commutative property refers to the ability to change the order of an addition or a multiplication expression without affecting the value of the expression.

Use the commutative property to rewrite and solve each expression.

Example

3×4 is the same as $4 \times 3 = 12$.

1. 2×3 is the same as ________ = ________.
2. $\frac{1}{4} + \frac{1}{5}$ is the same as ________ = ________

The associative property comes from the Latin prefix *as-* which means "with" and the root *soci* which means "partner".

Associative property refers to the ability to change the grouping of an addition or a multiplication expression without affecting the value of the expression.

Use the associative property to rewrite and solve each expression.

Example

$(2 \times 4) \times 3$ is the same as $2 \times (4 \times 3) = 24$.

3. $(400 \times 3) \times 2$ is the same as ______________ = ______________

4. $4.5 + (6.8 + 2.2)$ is the same as ______________ = ______________

11c Finding Surface Area from Nets

Example

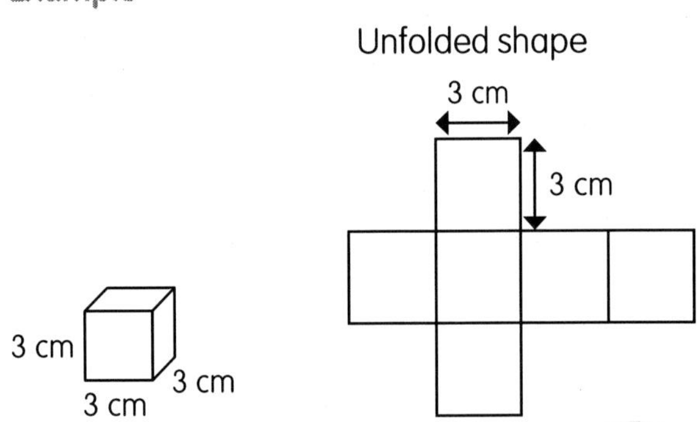

Area of one square face $= 3 \times 3$

$= 9 \text{ cm}^2$

Surface area of the cube $= 6 \times 9$

$= 54 \text{ cm}^2$

Surface area is the area of all the faces of a solid. You should know how to find the area of two-dimensional shapes. You can use that knowledge to find the surface area of a solid shape by visualizing the shape as a net of an unfolded solid.

1. Find the surface area of a cube with a side of 5 cm.

Area of one square face =

Surface area of the cube =

2

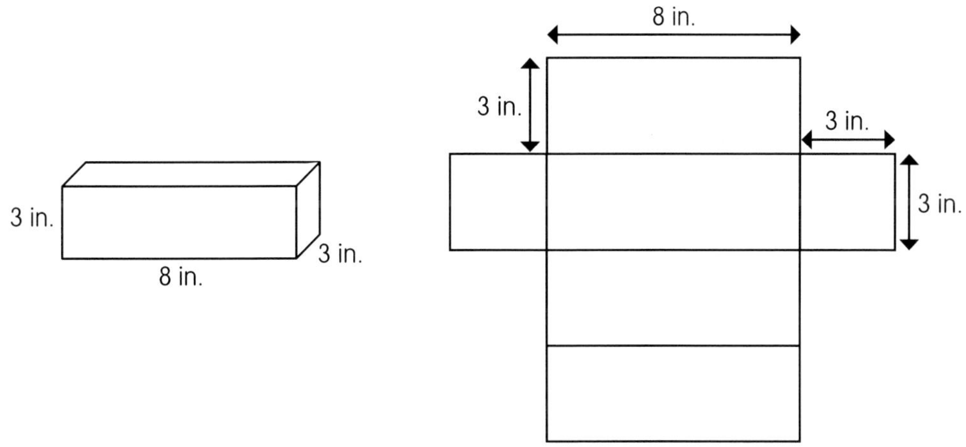

Find the surface area of a rectangular prism measuring 8 in. by 3 in. by 3 in.

Area of square base = ____________ in^2

Area of rectangle = ____________ in^2

Surface area of the prism = Area of square base × ____________ + Area of rectangle × ____________

=

Surface area of rectangular prism = ____________ in^2

11d Finding Surface Area from Nets

Find the surface area of the figures below. Label the nets to help you.

1

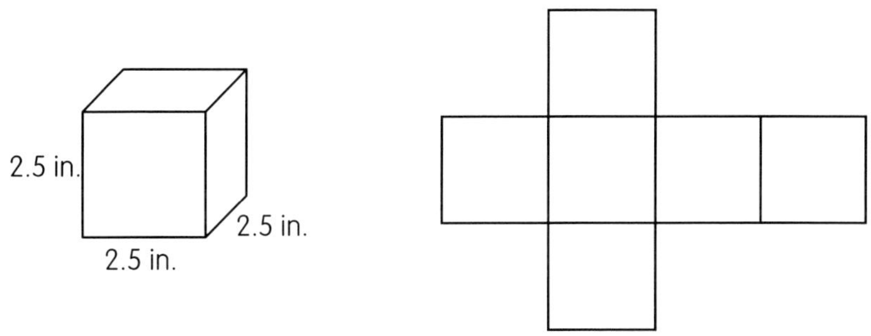

2

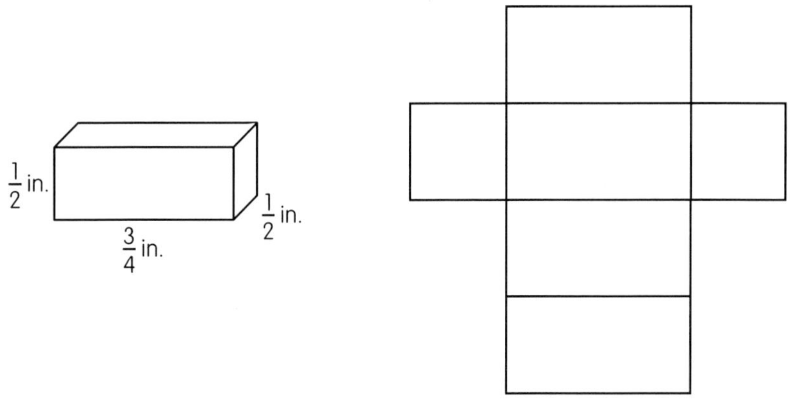

11e Real-World Surface Area Problems

Julia is building 5 rectangular wooden boxes for a project. She wants to paint the wooden boxes red. Each box must have the final dimensions of 3 ft. by 1.5 ft. by 1.5 ft.

1. Sketch the box below.

2. Sketch the net below.

3. If a can of red paint covers 50 square feet, how many cans of red paint will she need to buy to paint all the wooden boxes?

4. Explain your strategy to solve 3.

____

____

____

11f Finding Surface Area

Sketch each solid. Then, find its total surface area.

1. A cube of side of $\frac{1}{4}$ yd.

2. A box with dimensions of 11 in. by 6 in. by 6 in.

3. Two cubical toy boxes each with side of $7\frac{1}{2}$ in.

4. A refrigerator with dimensions of 30 in. by 30 in. by 70 in.

11g Finding Volume of a Rectangular Prism

Example

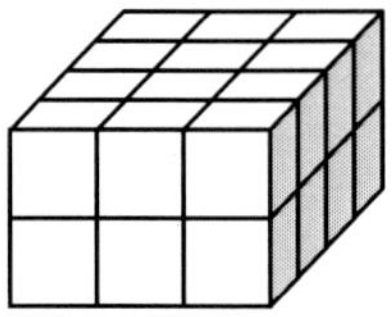

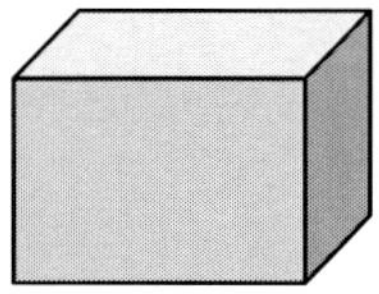

You can find volume by counting the number of cubes in the container.

By counting, 24 cubes can fit in the container.

So, the container has a volume of 24 cubic units or 24 units^3.

Another way to find volume is to multiply the area of the face of the rectangular prism by its depth.

Volume = **length × width × height**

= **3 × 4 × 2**

= **24 cubic units or units^3**

Find the volume.

1. 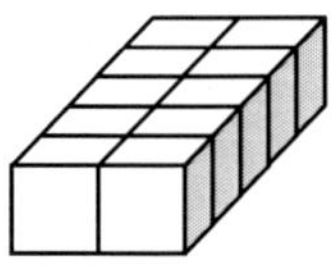

Volume =

2. 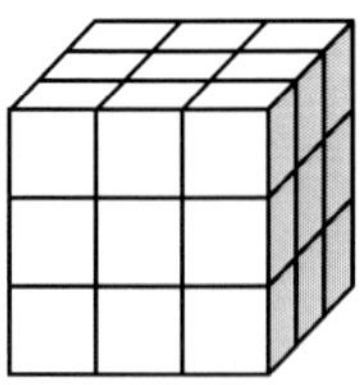

Volume =

11h Finding Volume of a Rectangle Prism

Complete the table.

Length of a rectangular prism	Width of a rectangular prism	Height of a rectangular prism	Volume of a rectangular prism
2 in.	3 in.	5 in.	
$\frac{1}{2}$ cm	$\frac{2}{3}$ cm	$\frac{1}{2}$ cm	
4.1 cm	0.5 cm	$\frac{7}{10}$ cm	
$\frac{1}{3}$ ft	1 ft		$\frac{1}{21}$ ft^3
	2.5 cm	1.25 cm	6.25 cm^3

11i Real-World Surface Area and Volume Problems

Solve. Show your work.

There is a new swimming pool in Greenwood estate. It measures 14 feet long by 28 feet wide by 6.5 feet deep.

1. Find the number of 1-ft^2 tiles needed to tile the sides and the bottom of the pool. Use a calculator to help you. Then, explain your thinking.

2. How many gallons of water would it take to fill up $\frac{3}{4}$ of the pool? Round your answer to the nearest gallon. Use a calculator to help you. Then, explain your thinking.

   (1 cubic foot = 7.38 gallons)

11j Area, Perimeter, Surface Area, and Volume

Compare area, perimeter, surface area, and volume.

1. Write three ways they are the same.

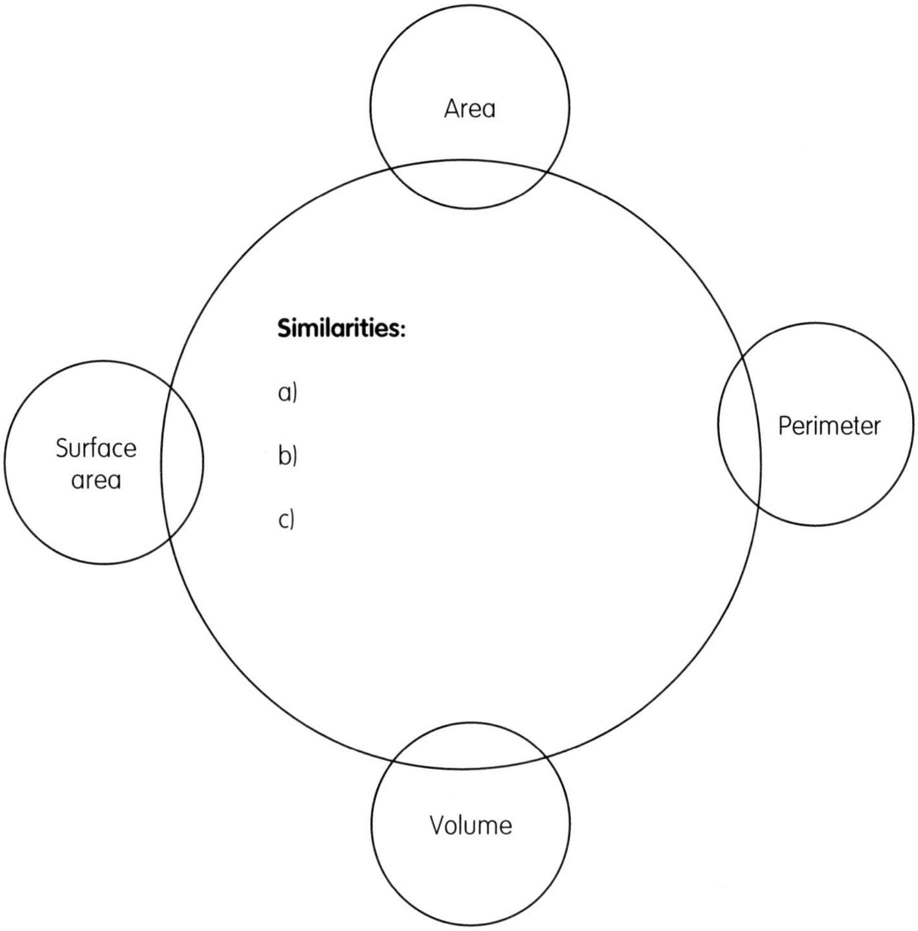

2. Write down their three differences.

____

____

____

____

____

Name: ______________________ Date: ____________

Chapter 12

Fact Fluency
More Practice on Ratio, Rate, and Percent

12a Finding Equivalent Ratios

Name the first ratio. Then, draw the model of an equivalent ratio and name the ratio you have drawn.

Example

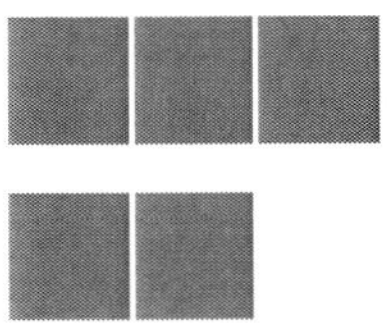
3 : 2

6 : 4

1. 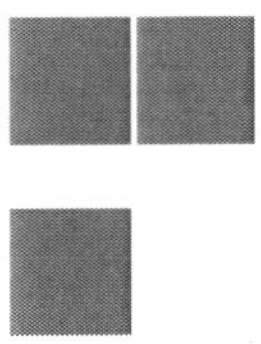 ________ : ________

2. 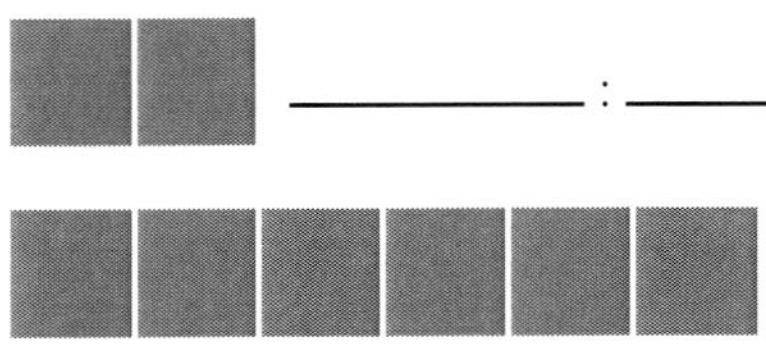 ________ : ________

Find an equivalent ratio to each given ratio.

3. 5 : 7 ________ : ________
4. 1 : 4 ________ : ________
5. 1.5 : 3 ________ : ________

12b Real-World Ratio and Change Problems

Solve. Show your work.

1. On a full flight from New York to Denver, the ratio of the number of passengers who had a window seat to the number of passengers who did not have a window seat was 2 : 3. During a stop in Chicago, some passengers who had the window seat got off and the ratio changed to 1 : 3. If there were 260 passengers on the plane at first, how many passengers were on the plane in the end?

2. If there were 12 window seats in first class, how many window seats were in economy class?

12c Finding Unit Rate

1. Find the **unit rate** for each item at the fruit stand:

Oranges: ____________ Apples: ____________

Grapes: ____________ Pineapple: ____________

2. Which fruit is the most inexpensive? Explain your thinking.

____

____

12d Real-World Unit Rate Problems

Runaway Bowling	Knockem Down Bowling
$29.99	✓ $4.99 per game
✓ for 2 hours of unlimited bowling	✓ Shoes are not included ($2.75 per person).
✓ includes shoe rental for up to 6 people	

Mike, Ken, and Susan want to go bowling. They will each play 3 games. Mike suggests going to Runaway Bowling because it will be less expensive per person. Susan says that they should go to Knockem Down because it will be less expensive per person.

1. Who is right?

____

____

____

2. Justify your answer.

____

____

____

12e Finding Percent

Solve.

1. 10% of 90 is ____________.
2. 25% of 120 is ____________.
3. 45 is 50% of ____________.
4. 80 is 20% of ____________.
5. 12 is ____________ percent of 48.
6. 9 is ____________ percent of 900.
7. 4.5% of 300 is ____________.
8. 0.1% of 100,000 is ____________.

12f Real-World Percent Problems

How common is your eye color?

It is estimated that 55% of the world's population have brown eyes. Of the total population, 8% have hazel eyes, 8% have blue eyes, and 2% have green eyes.

1. What percent of the world's population have eye colors other than brown, hazel, blue, or green? Show your thinking.

____

____

____

____

____

2. Using an estimated world's population of 7,633,000,000 people in 2018, complete the table below. Round to the nearest million. Use a calculator to help you.

Number of People with Each Eye Color in 2018

Brown: __________ Hazel: __________

Blue: __________ Green: __________

Others: __________

3. Why does the total not equal 7,633,000,000?

____

____

12g Ratio, Rate, and Percent

1. How are ratio, unit rate, and percent alike?

2. How are ratio, unit rate, and percent different?

3. Create a real-world problem in which finding the ratio is a better way to express your answer than finding the percent. Then, find the solution.

4. Why do you think ratio is the best way to express the answer to your problem?

Name: ____________________ Date: ____________

Chapter 13

Fact Fluency
Statistics

13a Finding Mean

Example

Jason, Ella, and Grace are collecting shells at the beach.

Jason collects 9 shells, Ella collects 3 shells, and Grace collects 6 shells.

They put the shells in a bucket to carry home.

When they reach home, they decide to share the shells equally.

How many shells will each of them get?

9 + 3 + 6 = 18
18 shells ÷ 3 children = 6 shells

6 is the mean or average number of shells each child will receive.

Statistics is the study of data. Mean is the arithmetic average of a set of data points.

1. During a basketball game, Evan scored 14 points, Jacob scored 22 points, and Lucas scored 6 points. What is the mean number of points scored by the three players? Show your work.

   Step 1: Find the total number of points scored. ____________

   Step 2: Divide by the number of players. ____________

   The mean number of points scored by the three players is ____________.

2. In your own words, describe what finding the mean of a set of data represents.

   ____

   ____

13b Finding Mean

Find the mean of each set of data. Use a calculator to help you.

1. 9, 4, 8

2. 7, 3, 7, 3

3. 5, 9, 3, 13

4. $\frac{1}{2}$, $\frac{1}{4}$, $\frac{1}{2}$, $\frac{3}{4}$, 2, 2

5. 3.2, 4.5, 14.02, 9.04

6. $5\frac{1}{2}$, 6.4, 3, 1.75, 2

7. Sofia received the following scores on her essays in Social Studies throughout the year: 85, 90, 82, 93, 95. What is her mean score? Show your work.

8. In order to get an "A" in Social Studies, Sofia has to get an average of 90 points on her essays. What is the minimum score she must get on her next essay to receive an "A"?

13c Finding Mean, Median, and Mode

Example

A shoe store has the following sizes of shoes available:
7, 9, 9, 9, 10, 10, 11,11, 12.

9 is the mode of the sizes as it appears most frequently.

10 is the median of the sizes as it is the value in the middle of the data set.

Mode is the most frequent value that appears in a set of data.

Median is the value or values in the middle of a set of data.

Pedro placed 7 containers in his neighborhood to collect rainwater after a recent storm. He collected the following amounts of rainwater in inches: 2, 3, 2, 3, 4, 4, 3.

1. Find the mean amount of rainwater he collected.

2. Find the mode amount of rainwater he collected.

3. Find the median amount of rainwater he collected.
(Hint: Sometimes it is necessary to put the data in a numerical order to calculate the median.)

13d Finding Mean, Median, and Mode

Find the mean, median, and mode of each data set. Use a calculator to help you.

1. Cole measured his heart rate 5 times on his bike ride.
He got the following heart rate readings in beats per minute: 80, 83, 83, 87, 101.

Mean: ____________ Median: ____________ Mode: ____________

2. Rachel went bowling. She scored the following in three games: 92, 101, 76.

Mean: ____________ Median: ____________ Mode: ____________

3 Susan kept track of the daily lowest temperature in degree Celsius in Detroit, Michigan for seven days.

Monday	Tuesday	Wednesday	Thursday	Friday	Saturday	Sunday
−1°C	−8°C	−10°C	−6°C	−11°C	−12°C	−10°C

Mean: ____________ Median: ____________ Mode: ____________

13e Measure of Central Tendency

The table shows the number of servings of fruit and vegetables that 22 first-graders ate in one day.

Servings of fruit and vegetables in one day	Tally
1	𝍸
2	|||
3	𝍸 ||
4	𝍸 ||

Mean, median, and mode are often called **measures of central tendency** because they give us information about the center of a set of data.

Find the mean, median, and mode of the data set.
(Hint: It is important to consider the frequency of a data point. In the first row, you can see that the tally shows us that 5 first-graders ate 1 serving of fruit and vegetables. To calculate the measures of central tendency, it is helpful to write out in this way: 1,1,1,1,1.)

Mean: ____________ Median: ____________ Mode: ____________

13f Measure of Spread

Measure of spread tells us about the variation in a set of data. You can use a graph to measure the spread of a set of data. A dot plot is created based on the information in **13e**.

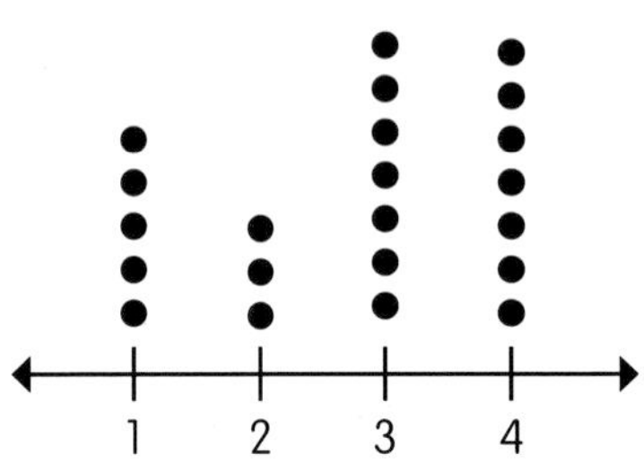

1. What do you notice about the dot plot?

____

____

2. When the data leans to one side in the dot plot, the shape of the dot plot is **skewed**. Explain what it means when the data is skewed.

____

____

3. How would looking at the mean, median, and mode tell you about the skewed distribution?

____

____

13g Finding Quartiles

When finding the median, you are finding the exact center of a group of data points.

1. Find the median of the following set of data points: 3, 4, 5, 6, 5, 7, 5, 7, 6, 3, 2, 1.

Median ____________

After putting the scores in ascending numerical order, you can also find the median in the quartiles of a data set.

2. Find the median of the lower half of the data in 1: ____________

3. Find the median of the upper half of the data in 1: ____________

4. Using the same set of data points in 1, complete the graph.

1st quartile | 2nd quartile | 3rd quartile | 4th quartile

Median of lower half = ________

Median = ________

Median of upper half = ________

13h Finding Mean Absolute Deviation

Mean Absolute Deviation (MAD) is the average distance of all the data points from the mean.

MAD is useful in telling us how close the data points are from the mean.

Example

The legal voting age in ten South American countries is:
16, 18, 16, 18, 18, 18, 18, 18, 18, 17.

$$\text{Mean} = \frac{16 + 18 + 16 + 18 + 18 + 18 + 18 + 18 + 18 + 17}{10}$$

$= 17.5$ years old

Find the distance of each data point (16, 17, 18) from the mean.

16 is 1.5 years from the mean.
18 is 0.5 years from the mean.
17 is 0.5 years from the mean.

Add all of the distances and divide the sum by the number of data points to get the MAD.

$$\text{MAD} = \frac{1.5 + 0.5 + 1.5 + 0.5 + 0.5 + 0.5 + 0.5 + 0.5 + 0.5 + 0.5}{10}$$

MAD = 0.7

The average life expectancy of twelve breeds of dogs is: 6, 7, 9, 9, 10, 10, 10, 12, 13, 14, 16, 17.

1. Calculate the mean.

2. Calculate the mean absolute deviation.

3. What does the mean absolute deviation tell you?

13i Real-World Statistics Problems

Conduct a survey with ten students in your class on a topic with a numerical answer.
(Hint: You can conduct a survey on their shoe sizes, the number of pets they own or how many siblings they have or another topic you choose.)

Survey title: ____________________

Name of student	Answer

13j Real-World Statistics Problems

1. Using the data in the survey above to find

   Mean: __________ Median: __________ Mode: __________

2. The range is the distance from the largest to the smallest data point. Find the range.

3. The interquartile range is the distance from the lowest to the upper quartiles. Find the interquartile range.

4. Find the mean absolute deviation.

5. Write three conclusions you can draw about the data set in your survey.

13k Statistics

Studying statistics helps people make important decisions in everything from sports to banking to healthcare.

1. Give three specific examples of when statistics are important to you.

2. What information can you gather from each of these examples?

3. How does the information you gather help you in making a decision?

Answers

Chapter 1

1a

1. 42
2. 7
3. 72
4. 8
5. 27
6. 4
7. 56
8. 36
9. 6
10. 6
11. 49
12. 81
13. 5
14. 3
15. Listing the factors.

1b

1. 9
2. 8
3. 8
4. 9
5. 6
6. 3
7. 9
8. 7
9. 8
10. 7
11. 8
12. 7
13. 1; 1
14. Answers vary.
    Example: If $25 \div 5 \div 5 = 1$, then $16 \div 4 \div 4 = 1$.

1c

1. Prime
2. Composite; 2 or 3 or 4 or 6 or 8 or 9
3. Composite; 3
4. Composite; 3 or 9
5. 2, 3, 5, 7, 11, 13, 17, 19, 23, 29
6. Divisibility rules of 2, 3, 4, 6 and 7
7. Divisibility rule of 11

1d

1. Answers vary. Example:

2	240
2	120
3	60
5	20
2	4
	2

$240 = 2 \times 2 \times 2 \times 2 \times 3 \times 5$

2. Answers vary. Example:
   I used the factor ladder method. I chose the method because it is similar to the work of division. It helped me to work out the answer easily.

1e

1. 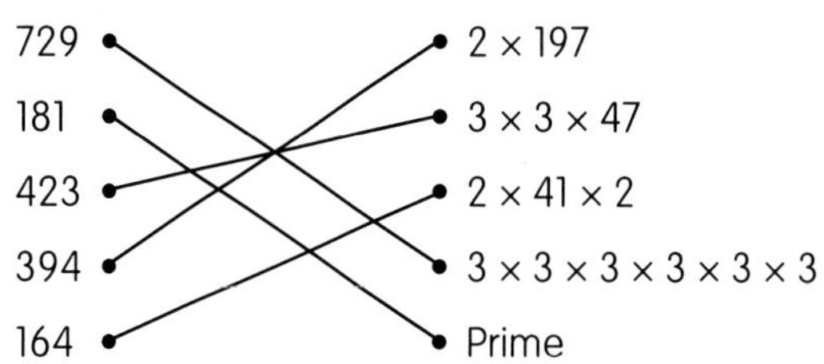

2. Yes, I noticed some large prime factors such as 41, 47, and 197. They are prime factors because each number has two factors, 1 and itself.

1f

1. 14,839 = 11 × 19 × 71
   5,593 = 7 × 17 × 47
   1,562 = 2 × 11 × 71
   209,291 = 47 × 61 × 73
   13,409 = 11 × 23 × 53
2. The dog ate our pie.

1g

No, I don't agree with Adam's thinking. The common multiple of 2, 3, 5, and 7 is 210. Hence, all four lights will flash at 210 seconds.

Chapter 2

2a

1. 21; 21; 21; 21
2. 56; 56; 8; 56; 7; 56
3. 48; 96; 24
4. 6; 3; 30
5. Answers will vary. Example:
   The related facts help me use common factors in getting the answers quickly.
   6 × 8 = 48;
   12 × 8 = 2 × 6 × 8
   = 2 × 48
   = 96

2b

1. 40
2. 42
3. 4
4. 9
5. 7
6. 56
7. 8
8. 21
9. 7
10. 32
11. 9
12. 18
13. True
    36 × 6 = 216
    Using distributive property,
    (30 × 6) + (6 × 6) = 180 + 36
    = 216
    Answers vary. Example:
    54 × 9 = (50 × 9) + (4 × 9)

2c

1. 135; 1350; 1485
2. 936; 10,920; 11,856
3. 492
4. 10,132
5. 7,245
6. 13
7. 20
8. 227
9. 231
10. 81
11. 8,004

2d

1. 32 × 45 = 1,440; 1440 cans
2. 1,440 ÷ 14 = 102 R 12; 102 food bags
3. 102 × 4 = 408 packets of tuna;
   102 × 2 = 204 boxes of cereal;
   102 × 3 = 306 bags of spaghetti.

2e

1. 17
2. 76
3. 4
4. 8

2f

1. +; ÷; 60
2. ÷; −; 30
3. ÷; +; −; 11
4. +; ÷; −; 14
5. Answers vary. Example:
   The number is 68.
   36 − 18 ÷ 3 × 2 + 44 = 68

2g

1. Using \$15 discount coupon,
   \$35 – \$15 = \$20
   \$20 + \$12 = \$32
   Using \$10 discount coupon,
   \$35 + \$12 = \$47
   \$47 – \$10 = \$37
   Matthew should use the \$15 discount coupon.
2. Matthew will have to pay \$32 if he uses the least expensive way.
3. \$32 + \$12 = \$44
   \$44 – \$10 = \$34
   Matthew will have to pay \$34 if he buys the blue jeans.
   Matthew should buy the black jeans if he wants to pay the least possible amount.

2h

1. 4 adults and 24 students
2. (4 × \$18) + (24 × \$12) = \$360

2i

Answers vary.

Chapter 3

3a

1. 6; 4; 10; 50
2. 3; 6; 9; 90
3. 9; 3; 24; 6
4. 16
5. 4
6. 6
7. 20

3b

1. 2; $\frac{3}{6}$; $\frac{1}{2}$
2. 6; $\frac{9}{10}$
3. $\frac{1}{4} + \frac{1}{4} = \frac{2}{4}$
4. $\frac{2}{6} + \frac{3}{6} = \frac{5}{6}$
5. $\frac{5}{15} + \frac{9}{15} = \frac{14}{15}$
6. $\frac{16}{56} + \frac{21}{56} = \frac{37}{56}$
7. $\frac{5}{15} - \frac{3}{15} = \frac{2}{15}$
8. $\frac{4}{6} - \frac{3}{6} = \frac{1}{6}$
9. $\frac{10}{14} - \frac{7}{14} = \frac{3}{14}$
10. $\frac{8}{12} - \frac{3}{12} = \frac{5}{12}$

3c

1. $\frac{2}{4}$ or $\frac{1}{2}$

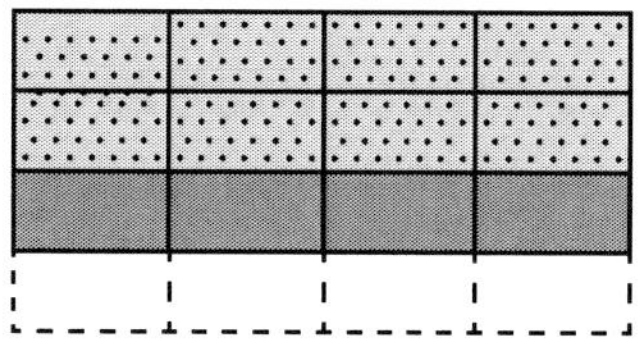

2. $\frac{1}{10}$

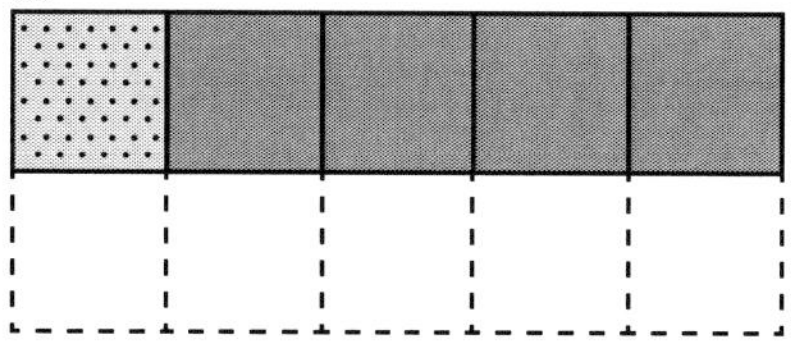

3. $\frac{3}{10}$
4. $\frac{1}{25}$
5. $\frac{1}{28}$
6. $\frac{1}{9}$
7. $\frac{3}{16}$
8. $\frac{9}{100}$

3d

1. 12

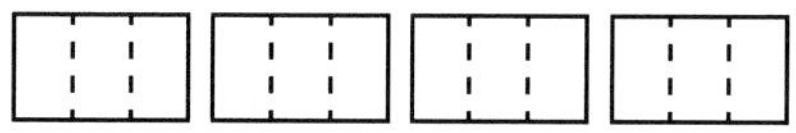

2. 12

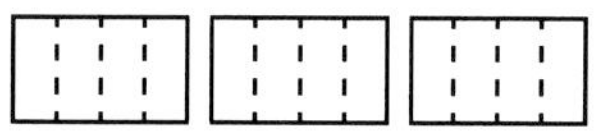

3. $\frac{1}{12}$

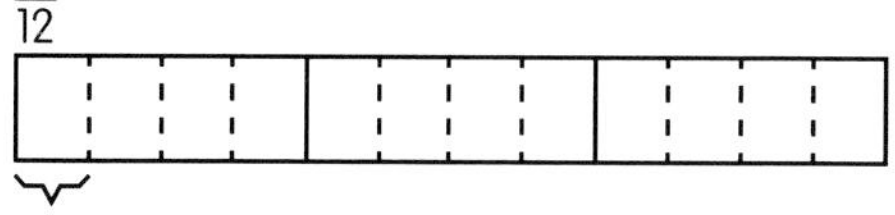

$\frac{1}{12}$

4. $\frac{2}{15}$

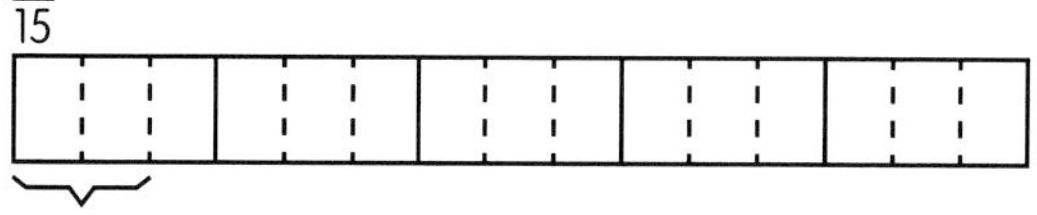

$\frac{2}{15}$

3e

1. 9; 18; 27
2. $\frac{1}{9}, \frac{1}{18}, \frac{1}{27}$
3. $\frac{2}{9}, \frac{1}{9}, \frac{2}{27}$
4. Answers vary. Example:
   When dividing fractions, it is the same as multiplying the whole number or fraction by the reciprocal of the divisor.

   $3 \div \frac{1}{3} = 3 \times \frac{3}{1} = 9$ and

   $\frac{1}{3} \div 3 = \frac{1}{3} \times \frac{1}{3} = \frac{1}{9}$.

3f

$1\frac{1}{2}$

Method 1:

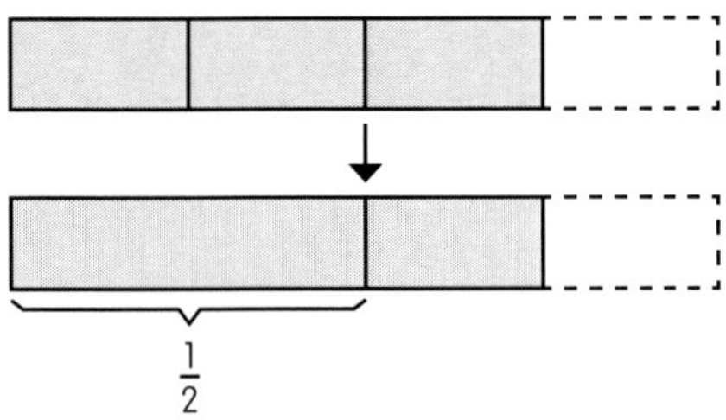

Method 2:

$$\begin{aligned} \frac{3}{4} \div \frac{1}{2} &= \frac{3}{4} \times \frac{2}{1} \\ &= \frac{6}{4} \\ &= \frac{3}{2} \\ &= 1\frac{1}{2} \end{aligned}$$

3g

1. $\frac{1}{2}$
2. $\frac{3}{4}$
3. $\frac{4}{5}$
4. $\frac{9}{8}$ or $1\frac{1}{8}$
5. $\frac{8}{7}$ or $1\frac{1}{7}$
6. $\frac{3}{2}$ or $1\frac{1}{2}$
7. 1
8. 3
9. 1
10. Answers vary. Example:
    When the divisor is larger than the dividend, the answer is a fraction. When the divisor is smaller than the dividend, the answer is an improper fraction or a mixed number. When the divisor is equivalent to the dividend, the answer is 1.

3h

1. 0.09
2. 0.8
3. 0.35
4. 1.5
5. 3.2
6. 0.75
7. $\frac{3}{10}$
8. $\frac{23}{25}$
9. $\frac{1}{25}$
10. $\frac{29}{200}$
11. $2\frac{4}{5}$
12. $4\frac{4}{125}$

3i

1. 7.7
2. 8.31
3. 0.19
4. 0.888
5. 0; 3
6. 9
7. 2
8. Answers vary. Example:

$$\begin{array}{rcccccc} & 5 & 1 & . & 2 & 4 & \\ - & & 9 & . & 0 & \square & 5 \\ \hline & 4 & 2 & . & 1 & 5 & 5 \end{array}$$

3j

1. 10; $\frac{20}{100}$; 0.2
2. $\frac{12}{100}$; $\frac{54}{10}$; $\frac{648}{1,000}$; 0.648

3. $\frac{306}{1,000}$; 0.306

4. $\frac{92}{100}$; $\frac{3}{100}$; $\frac{276}{10,000}$; 0.0276

3k

1. $\frac{34}{100}$
2. $\frac{43}{1,000}$
3. $\frac{67}{10}$
4. $\frac{100}{4}$; $\frac{200}{40} = 5$
5. $\frac{1}{5}$
6. 150
7. 8
8. 1.5
9. 1.4

3l

1. 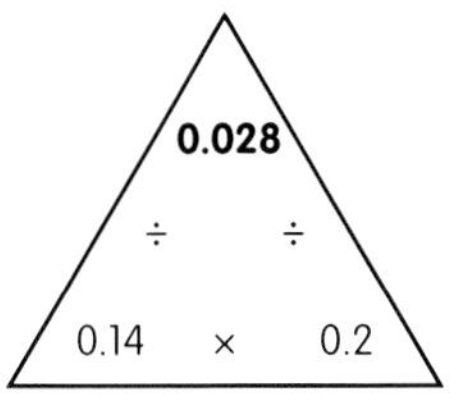

2. 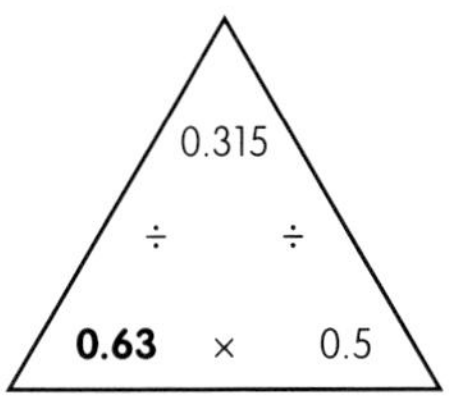

3. 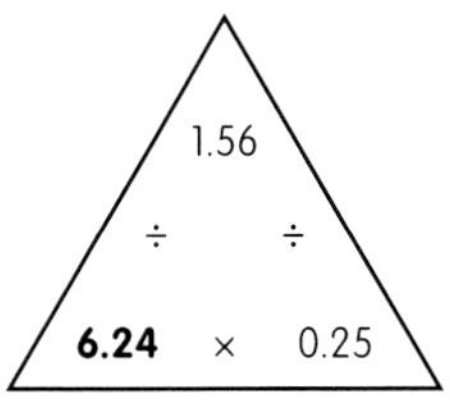

4. 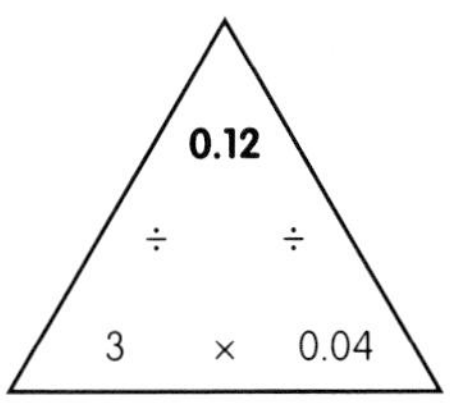

5. 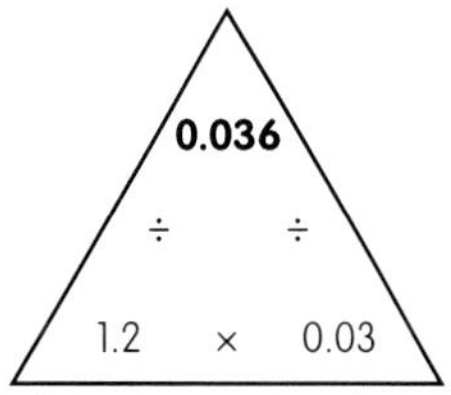

3m

D	C	B	A
10.48	14.98	15.72	26.2

3n

1. Answers vary. Example:
Grace has a better argument.

2. Answers vary. Example: Rewriting decimals to fractions and adding all fractions together is easier.

3. Zachary's strategy:

$$\frac{1}{2} + 0.4 + \frac{3}{5} + \left(\frac{2}{5} \times \frac{4}{10}\right) + \left(0.2 \times \frac{1}{3}\right)$$
$$= 0.5 + 0.4 + 0.6 + (0.4 \times 0.4) + (0.2 \times 0.\overline{3})$$
$$= 0.5 + 0.4 + 0.6 + 0.16 + 0.0\overline{6}$$
$$= 1.72\overline{6}$$

Grace's strategy:

$$= \frac{1}{2} + 0.4 + \frac{3}{5} + \left(\frac{2}{5} \times \frac{4}{10}\right) + \left(0.2 \times \frac{1}{3}\right)$$
$$= \frac{1}{2} + \frac{4}{10} + \frac{3}{5} + \left(\frac{2}{5} \times \frac{4}{10}\right) + \left(\frac{1}{5} \times \frac{1}{3}\right)$$
$$= \frac{1}{2} + \frac{4}{10} + \frac{3}{5} + \frac{4}{25} + \frac{1}{15}$$
$$= 1\frac{109}{150}$$

Chapter 4

4a

1. $\frac{6}{8}$, $\frac{9}{12}$, $\frac{75}{100}$, $\frac{30}{40}$
2. $\frac{4}{10}$, $\frac{16}{40}$, $\frac{40}{100}$, $\frac{800}{2,000}$
3. $\frac{88}{100}$, $\frac{44}{50}$, $\frac{3,520}{4,000}$

4. Answers vary. Examples: $\frac{3}{9}, \frac{4}{12}, \frac{5}{15}$

5. Answers vary. Examples: $\frac{3}{5}, \frac{9}{15}, \frac{12}{20}$

4b

1. Answers vary. Example:
   $\frac{50}{200}, \frac{25}{100}, \frac{5}{20}, \frac{1}{4}$
2. Answers vary. Example:
   $\frac{12}{30}, \frac{6}{15}, \frac{2}{5}$
3. Answers vary. Example: $\frac{115}{1{,}250}, \frac{23}{250}$

4c

1. Starting from the bottom,

   6th row of the pyramid: $\frac{2}{5}; \frac{3}{4}$

   5th row of the pyramid: $\frac{3}{10}; \frac{3}{5}; \frac{3}{10}$

   4th row of the pyramid: $\frac{3}{50}; \frac{9}{50}$

   3rd row of the pyramid: $\frac{27}{2{,}500}$

   2nd row of the pyramid: $\frac{2{,}187}{6{,}250{,}000}$

   1st row of the pyramid: $\frac{531{,}441}{39{,}062{,}500{,}000{,}000}$
2. Answers vary.

4d

1. 8: 4 or 2: 1
2. 4: 8 or 1: 2
3. 8: 12 or 2: 3

4e

1. 12
2. 4
3. 12 : 3; 4 : 1

4f

1. 1
2. 4
3. 75
4. 2 : 6; 3 : 9; 4 : 12
5. 4 : 10; 6 : 15; 8 : 20
6. 25 : 1
7. 2 : 1
8. 7 : 3
9. The two methods for finding equivalent ratios are multiplication and division.

4g

1. 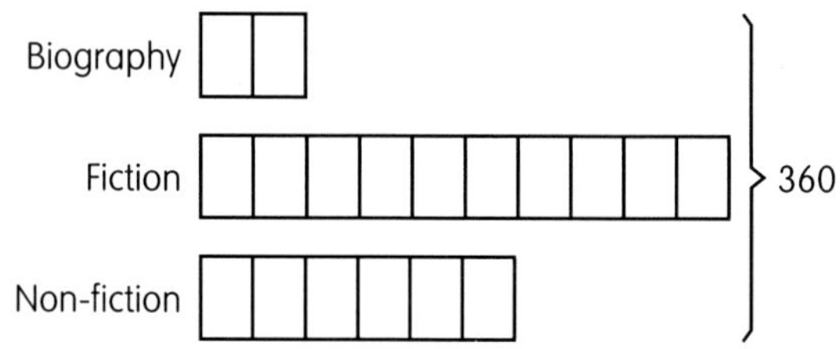

2. 200
3. 120
4. 40

4h

6 teaspoons of olive oil, 30 teaspoons of coconut milk, 192 teaspoons of chicken stock; 96 teaspoons of water

4i

1. Bed: $1\frac{1}{2} \times 3$

   Desk: $2 \times 1\frac{1}{4}$

   Chair: 1×1

   Cupboard: 4×6

   Bookshelf: $\frac{1}{2} \times \frac{1}{2}$
2. Answers vary. Example:
   Desk
   Actual dimensions: 48×30
   Model dimensions: $2 \times 1\frac{1}{4}$

4j

1. Answers vary. Example:
   Raj and Ella collected some money at a fundraising event. The ratio of the amount of money collected by Raj to the amount of money collected by Ella was 4 : 3. They collected $2,100 altogether.

   a How much did Raj collect?

   b How much did Ella collect?

   c How much more did Raj collect than Ella?

(2) 7 units = \$2,100
1 unit = \$2,100 ÷ 7
= \$300
4 units = \$300 × 4
= \$1,200
Raj collected \$1,200.

3 units = \$300 × 3
= \$900
Ella collected \$900.

\$1,200 – \$900 = \$300
Raj collected \$300 more than Ella.

4k

Answers vary. Example:
Yes, I agree with Jonathan.
When there are more than 2 items, the ratio cannot be written as a fraction.
The example below shows that a ratio cannot be written as a fraction.

In the part-part model below,

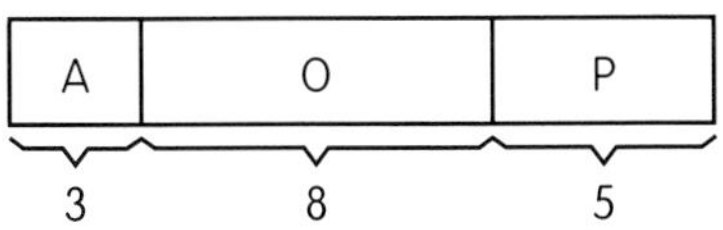

A: Apple   O: Orange   P: Pears

The ratio of the number of apples to the number of oranges to the number of pears, 3 : 8 : 5, cannot be written in fraction.

Chapter 5

5a

(1) $\frac{4}{6}$ or $\frac{2}{3}$

(2) $\frac{2}{6}$ or $\frac{1}{3}$

(3) $\frac{1}{6}$

(4) $\frac{2}{6}$ or $\frac{1}{3}$

(5) $\frac{6}{6}$ or 1

5b

(1) $\frac{3}{8}, \frac{2}{8}$ or $\frac{1}{4}, \frac{3}{8}$

(2) 6

(3) $3 \div \frac{1}{2} = 6$

(4) 6

(5) $2 \div \frac{1}{3} = 6$

(6) 2

(7) $\frac{3}{2}$ or $1\frac{1}{2}$

5c

(1) 15

(2) $7\frac{1}{2}$

(3) $\frac{3}{10}$

(4) 30

(5) 10

(6) $\frac{1}{10}$

(7) 45

(8) $6\frac{3}{7}$

(9) $\frac{7}{45}$

5d

(1) 3 minutes

(2) A unit rate is a ratio that compares a quantity to one unit of a different quantity.

(3) Rate and ratio are used for comparison. Rate can compare two quantities with different units but ratio compares two quantities with the same unit.

5e

(1) 0.50

(2) 30

(3) 8

(4) 10.05

5f

(1) \$0.28
\$0.18
\$0.11
\$0.09

(2) Trademark Kitchen was the least expensive in terms of price per ounce.

3. Answers vary. Example: Yes, I would assume that the Silver Star would be the most expensive while the Cousin Ben the cheapest. After calculating their unit rate, Cousin Ben turns out to be the most expensive and Trademark Kitchen the cheapest.

5g

1. 0.2
2. 16

5h

1.

Emma	Running	41
Kayla	Running	39
Paige	Running	42
Emma	Swimming	24
Kayla	Swimming	40
Paige	Swimming	30
Emma	Biking	100
Kayla	Biking	93
Paige	Biking	92

2. Kayla; 39 min
3. Emma
4. Paige; 164 min or 2 h 44 min

5i

1. $\frac{2}{10}$; $\frac{7}{10}$; 14; 0.14
2. $\frac{4}{100}$; $\frac{5}{10}$; 20; 0.02
3. $\frac{12}{10}$; $\frac{7}{10}$; $\frac{84}{100}$; 0.84
4. 0.036
5. 0.004
6. 5.85
7. 6.868
8. 0.021
9. 12.108

5j

1.

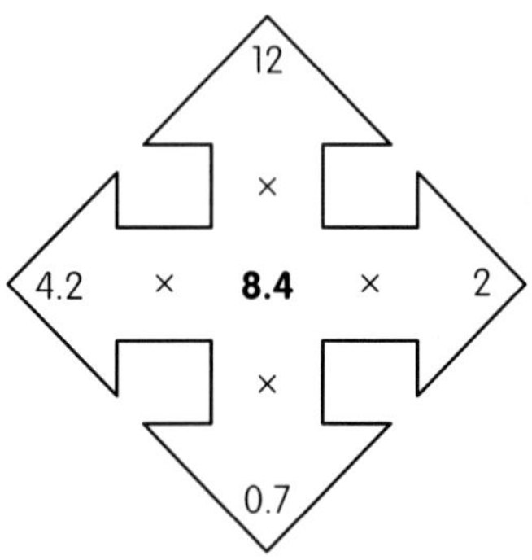

2.

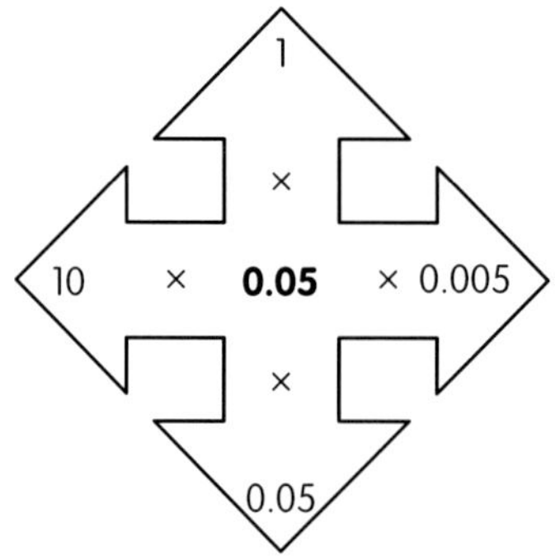

3.

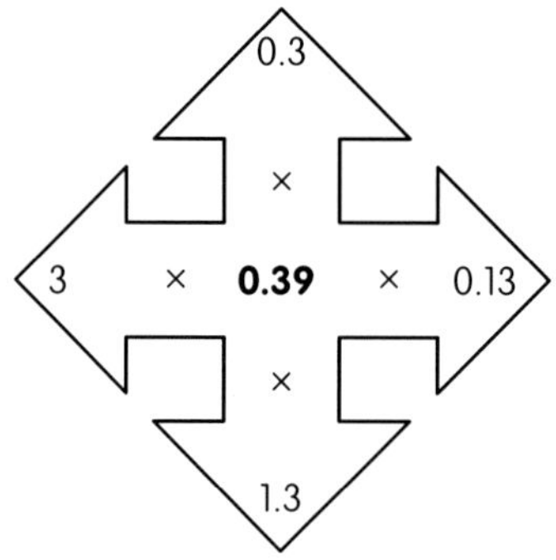

5k

1. 45 miles
2. 50 minutes/$\frac{5}{6}$ hour
3. 54 mi/h

5l

Total distance
= 262 + 504 + 235 + 376
= 1,377 miles

Total drive time
= 4 h 30 min + 8 h 30 min
+ 4 h 45 min + 6 h 15 min
= 22 h 120 min
= 24 h

Average rate
= Total distance ÷ Total time
= 1,377 ÷ 24
= 57.375 mi/h

5m

1.

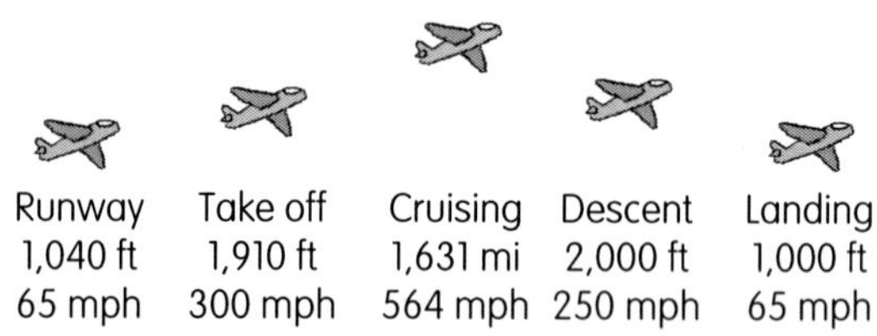

2. I would use the formula:
Average speed = Total distance ÷ Total time to find the average speed of the airplane.

3. Since 5,280 ft = 1 mi,
Distance = 1,040 ft = 0.20 mi
Time = 0.20 ÷ 65 = 0.003 h

Distance = 1,910 ft = 0.36 mi
Time = 0.36 ÷ 300 = 0.001 h

Distance = 2,000 ft = 0.38 mi
Time = 0.38 ÷ 250 = 0.002 h

Distance = 1,000 ft = 0.19 mi
Time = 0.19 ÷ 65 = 0.003 h

Total distance
= 0.20 + 0.36 + 1631 + 0.38 + 0.19
= 1,632.13 mi

1,631 mi ÷ 564 mph = 2.89 h

Total time
= 0.003 + 0.001 + 2.89 + 0.002 + 0.003
= 2.899 h

Average speed
= Total distance ÷ Total time
= 1,632.13 ÷ 2.899
= 563.0 mph

Chapter 6

6a

1. 6
2. 0.6
3. 0.06
4. 0.56
5. 0.056
6. 0.0056
7. 34
8. 0.34
9. 0.34
10. 20
11. 2
12. 0.2

6b

1. 4; 10; 40
2. 10; 25; 50
3. 1; 5; 25
4. 0.03; 1.5; 0.3

6c

1. 3
2. 34
3. 78
4. 13
5. 20
6. 1
7. $\frac{8}{25}$
8. $\frac{7}{50}$
9. $\frac{1}{20}$

6d

1. 56%
2. $\frac{8}{100}$
3. 0.17
4. $\frac{120}{100}$; 120%

6e

1. 4; 4
2. 16; 16
3. 65
4. 80
5. 10
6. 25
7. 2
8. 2

6f

1. 32 cups of apple juice, 45 cups of pineapple juice and 23 cups of orange juice
2. 67 students take the bus, 18 students walk to school and 15 students bike to school
3. 48% like Geometry, 28% like Algebra and 24% like Statistics

6g

1. 0.15;
   0.15; 6
2. 8
   8; 576
3. 62
   62; 589
4. $\frac{2}{100}$
   $\frac{2}{100}$; 1,400; 28

6h

1. 6
2. 2.4
3. 42
4. 138.7
5. 0.4
6. 247
7. 0.855
8. 0.42

6i

123.88
22.82
110.84
19.56
29.34
6.52
9.78
3.26

6j

1. 56%
2. 89%

6k

\$25 + \$16 + \$14 = \$55

If Connor uses Coupon 1,
25% off \$55 = \$13.75
\$55 – \$13.75 = \$41.25
he has to pay \$41.25.

If Connor uses Coupon 2,
\$55 – \$15 = \$40
he has to pay \$40.

Connor should use Coupon 2.

6l

1. 72
2. 81
3. 54
4. 56
5. 35
6. 42
7. 4
8. 6
9. 9
10. 7
11. 6
12. 7

6m

1. $180 \div 2 = 90$ ft^2
   $25\% \times 90 = 22.5$ ft^2
2. Answers vary.

Chapter 7

7a

1. $g + 8$
2. $g - 7$
3. 2:00 am on Feb 3rd 2019
4. 11 am

7b

1. 18; 21; 24; 27
2. 24; 32; 56; 68
3. 57
4. 121
5. 2
6. 6,342

7c

1. 6
2. 7
3. 8
4. 4

5 8

6 9

7 2

8 4

9 10

10

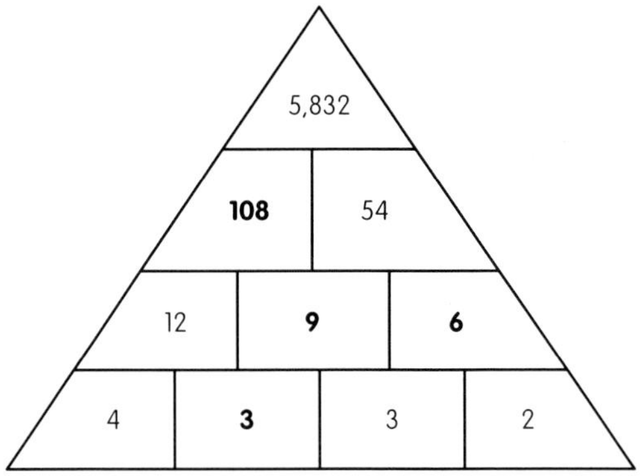

7d

1 9

2 8

3 9

4 5

5 9

6 8

7e

1 $a = 5$; $b = 3$; $c = 9$

2 $r = 5$; $p = 3$; $q = 2$

3 $x = 3$; $y = 4$

7f

1 1×24; 2×12; 3×8; 4×6

2 Answers vary. Example:
I worked from multiplication facts of 1 all the way to 4.

3 Answers vary. Example:
$21 \div 7$; $27 \div 9$, etc.

4 Answers vary. Example: When I started to list the division facts, I realized that there is an infinite list.

7g

1 a $2x$

b 400

2 a $4d$

b 600

7h

1 a $\frac{1}{2}j$ points

b 9 points

2 a $\frac{1}{5}t$

b 25

7i

1 21

2 4

3 8

7j

1 $4a$

2 $5b$

3 $\frac{1}{8}d$

4 $\frac{1}{4}d$

5 20

6 10

7k

1 1

2 1

3 1

4 $\frac{9}{10}$

5 $\frac{5}{8}$

6 $\frac{3}{4}$

7 $\frac{5}{6}$

8 $\frac{7}{10}$

9 $1\frac{1}{3}$

10 $\frac{5}{6}$

11 $\frac{11}{12}$

12 $1\frac{11}{20}$

7l

1 2.6

2 5.6

3. 0.13
4. 4
5. 8.9
6. 9.1
7. 2.81
8. 0.48
9. 0.038

7m

1. $\frac{1}{4}a$
2. $\frac{1}{2}t$
3. $\frac{2}{3}s$
4. 132
5. $\frac{1}{3}(a + r + t + s)$
6. 123

7n

1. 0.45p$
2. 1.20n$
3. 2.30b$
4. 0.80r$
5. $($2.30b + 0.80r)$
6. $5.40
7. Answers vary. Example:
   3($2.30) + 6($0.45)
   = $6.90 + $2.70
   = $9.60
   He could buy 3 notebooks and 6 pencils.

7o

1. Answers vary.
2. Answers vary.
3. Answers vary.

Chapter 8

8a

1. addition
2. subtraction
3. multiplication
4. division
5. equivalent; is the same as
6. $36 - 18 = 9 \times 2$
7. $2 + 2 + 2 = 19 - 13$
8. $4 \times 7 = 16 + 4 + 8$
9. $900 - 750 = 100 + 50$
10. $4.5 \times 2 = 18 \div 2$
11. $\frac{1}{2} + \frac{3}{4} = \frac{1}{4} \times 5$

8b

1. True; Both sides of equation equal 5.
2. False; 57 does not equal 37.
3. False; 3.5 does not equal 2.45.
4. False; $\frac{1}{2}$ does not equal 1.
5. False; 2.83 does not equal 0.

8c

1. Zara's height in inches; $t + 4$; $t - 3\frac{1}{2}$
2. temperature in San Francisco; $d + 9$; $d - 20$
3. amount of growth a tomato plant grows each day; $2x$; $\frac{1}{3}x$
4. distance Ana can run in 15 minutes; $m + 1$; $m + 1 + 0.8$

8d

1. number of pieces of rabbit treats
2. 10; 15
   16; 25
   5; 7
   20; 30
   5; 37
   4; 10

8e

1; 2; 9; 4; 3; 5; 6; 1; 8

I SOLVED IT!

8f

1. $3x = 2x + 6$
2. $2m = 4m - 6$

8g

1. 40; 64
2. $c = 8b$
3. 40; 100
4. $4n = p$

8h

1. $y = x + 7$
2. \$37
3. \$8
4. $t = x + (7 + x)$
5. James spent \$45 and Alex spent \$52.

8i

1. $5 < 10$
2. $17 > 5$
3. $27 < 45$ or $45 > 27$
4. $72 > 67$ or $67 < 72$
5. 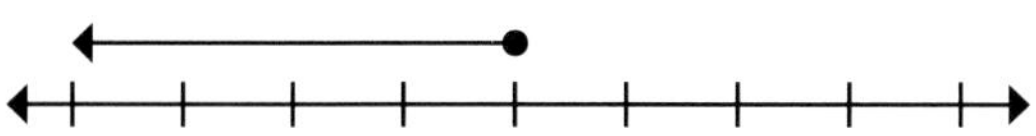

6. 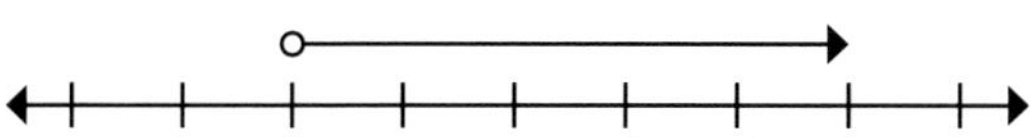

8j

1. $f \geq 8$
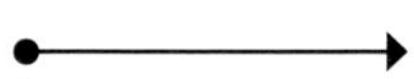

2. $d \leq \$10.25$

8k

1. at least 6 — $x \geq 6$
   more than 6 — $x > 6$
   at most 6 — $x \leq 6$
   less than 6 — $x < 6$
   between 3 and 6 — $3 \leq x \leq 6$
2. Answers vary.

8l

1. m = number of naked mole rats;
   $m \geq 25$
2. a = number of animals at the zoo;
   $a = 3500$
3. p = number of exotic plants;
   $p > 700{,}000$
4. l = length of a honey bee in inches;
   $l \leq 0.6$
5. f = length of an African dwarf crocodile in feet;
   $f < 5$

8m

1. 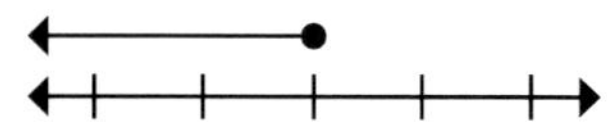

2. 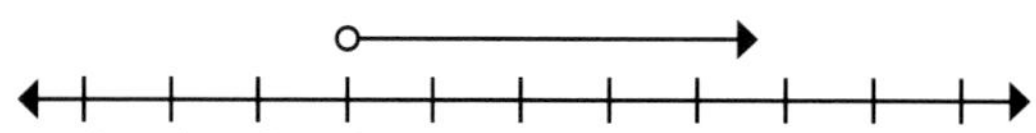

3. 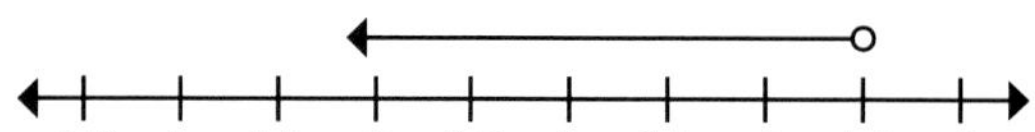

4. 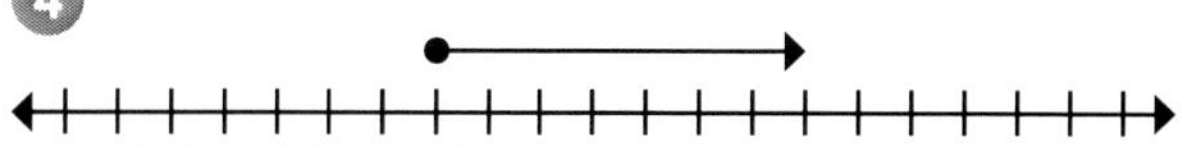

8n

1. $v \geq 3$
2. Yes, he could use more than three vans but they wouldn't be very full. The minimum is 3 vans.
3. No, values between the whole numbers are not valid solutions. Also, it is reasonable to assume that he would want the fewest vans possible.

8o

1. Numerical expression is a collection of numbers and operation symbols that represent a single value.
   Answers vary. Example: $4 \times 5 + 2$
2. Algebraic expression is an expression that contains at least one variable.
   Answers vary. Example: $6x + 3$
3. Algebraic equation is an equation that contains at least one algebraic expression.
   Answers vary. Example: $4y - 15 = 13$
4. Numerical inequality is a number sentence which states that two values are not equal.
   Answers vary. Example: $5 < 8$

5. Algebraic inequality is a number sentence which connects an algebraic expression to a value, variable or another expression which is not equal.
Answers vary. Example: $3 > x$

Chapter 9

9a

1. 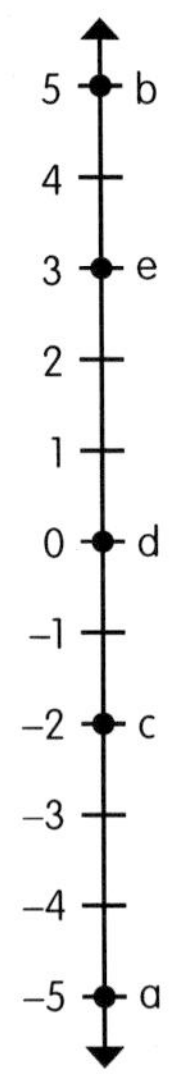

2. 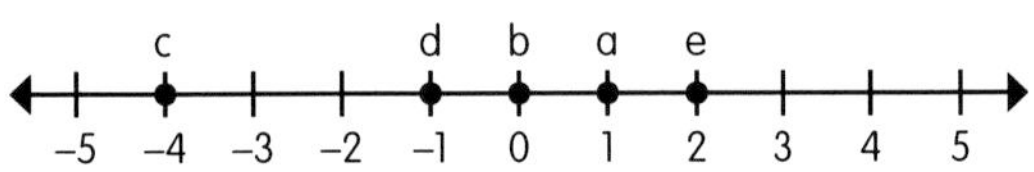

9b

1. D
2. E
3. B
4. C

9c

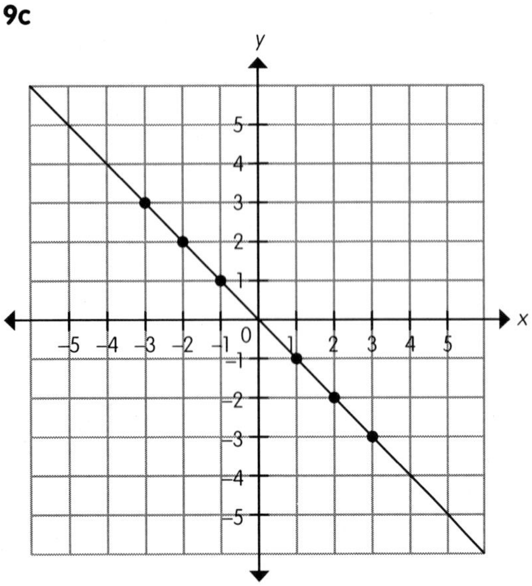

9d

1. 3
2. 5

9e

1. 7 ft
2. $31\frac{1}{2}$ cm
3. 12.08 in.
4. 26 cm
Answers vary. Example:
$2 + 9 + 2 + 4 + 4 + 5 = 26$ cm
or $30 - 4 = 26$ cm.

9f

3; 6; 3 ; 6
18 units

9g

1. Answers vary.
2. Answers vary.
3. Answers vary.

9h

1. Answers vary.
2. Answers vary.
3. Answers vary.
4. Answers vary.

Chapter 10

10a

1. 1
2. 15
3. $\frac{3}{4}$
4. $1\frac{3}{5}$
5. $9\frac{3}{5}$
6. $1\frac{5}{7}$
7. $\frac{1}{12}$
8. $\frac{1}{6}$
9. $\frac{1}{3}$
10. $\frac{3}{4}$

11. $\frac{8}{9}$
12. $1\frac{13}{20}$

10b

1. 10
2. 100
3. 235
4. 0.48 or $\frac{48}{100}$
5. $\frac{3}{10}$; 0.012 or $\frac{12}{1000}$
6. 5
7. 2
8. 1.5
9. 0.16
10. 0.004
11. 7.35

10c

1. a 15
   b 60
2. Answers vary. Example: One area is 4 times bigger than the other area.
3. a 9
   b $2\frac{1}{4}$
4. Answers vary. Example: Halving the sides reduced the answer by 4.

10d

7
6
42 cm^2
21 cm^2

10e

1. 56 in^2; 28 in^2
2. 8.05 cm^2; 4.025 cm^2
3. 30
4. $\frac{3}{16}$

10f

8 yd^2

10g

1. 27 ft^2
2. 16 in^2

10h

1. $7\frac{1}{2}$ cm^2
2. 63 in^2

10i

1. Area $= \frac{1}{2} \times (6.5 + 5) \times 9$
   $= 51.75$ in^2
2. $51.75 \times \$0.44 = \$22.77$

10j

1. 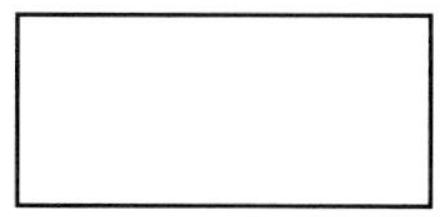
   $l \times h$
   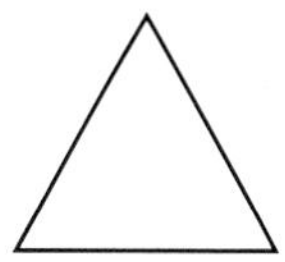
   $\frac{1}{2} \times b \times h$
   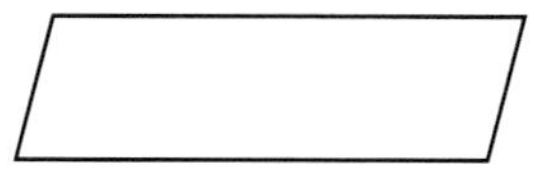
   $l \times h$
   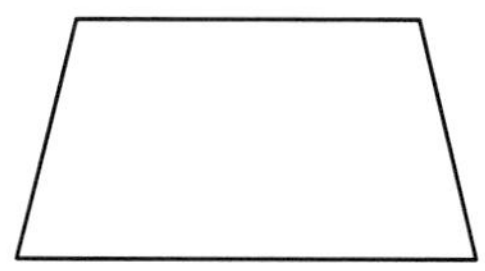
   $\frac{1}{2} \times h \times (b_1 + b_2)$
2. Answers vary. Example:
   All can be composed of triangles and rectangles.
3. 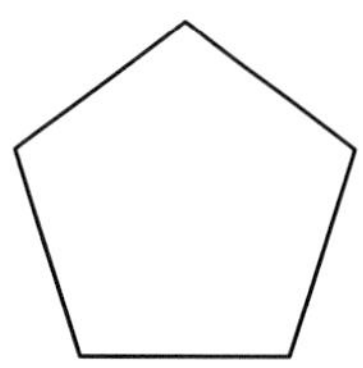
4. Answers vary. Example: Break it up into 5 equal triangles and find the area of one triangle then multiply by 5.

Chapter 11

11a

1. 2
2. 13

3 12

4 22

5 50

6 9

7 ×; +; −

8 +; ×; ÷

9 $4 \times (3 + 2) - 6 = 14$

10 $3 \times 3 \times (3 + 1) = 36$

11b

1 3×2; 6

2 $\frac{1}{5} + \frac{1}{4} = \frac{9}{20}$

3 $400 \times (3 \times 2)$; 2,400

4 $(4.5 + 6.8) + 2.2$; 13.5

11c

1 25cm²; 150 cm² → 25cm^2; 150 cm^2

2 9 in^2; 24 in^2;
2; 4; 114 in^2

11d

1 37.5 in^2

2 2 in^2

11e

1

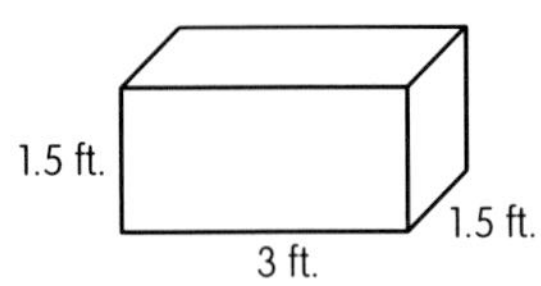

2

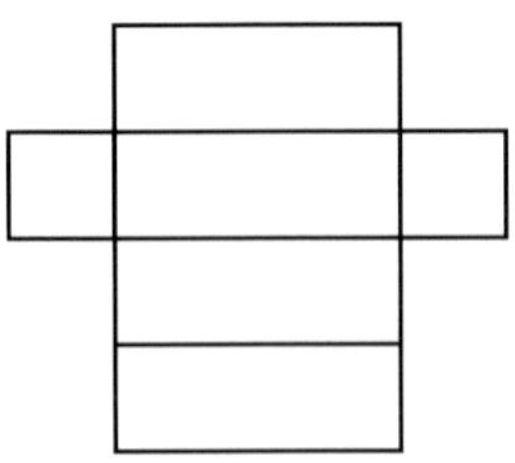

3 Total surface area = 112.5 ft^2
She will need 3 cans of red paint.

4 Answers vary. Example:
The total surface area of the 5 rectangular wooden boxes is 112.5 ft^2. Since a can of red paint covers 50 ft^2, 112.5 divided by 50 will give a result of 2.25. So, Julia needs 3 cans of paint.

11f

1

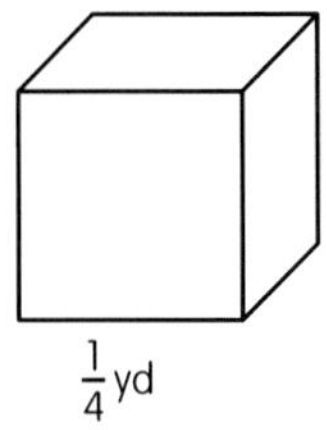

$\frac{3}{8}\text{ yd}^2$

2

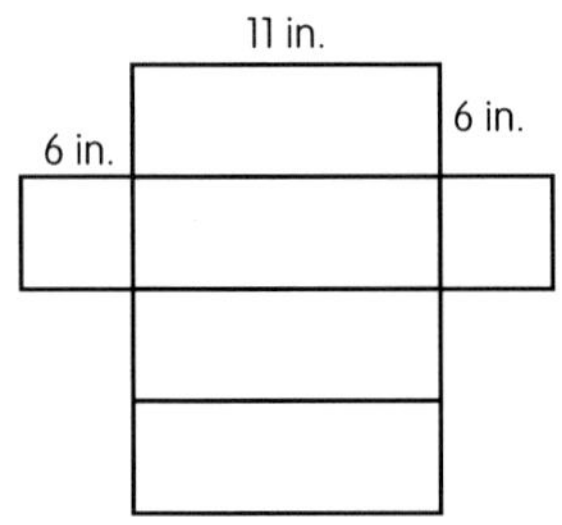

336 in^2

3

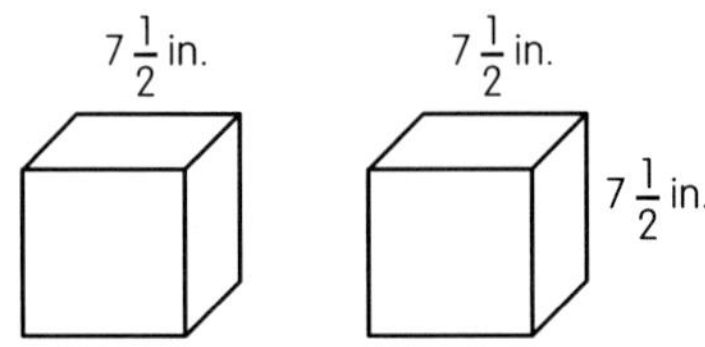

675 in^2

4

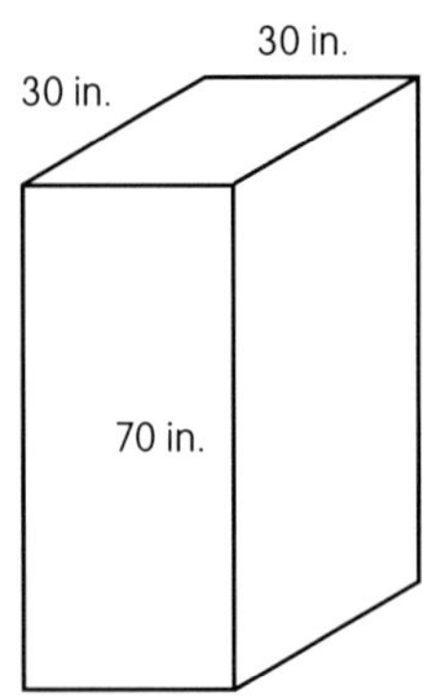

$10{,}200\text{ in}^2$

11g

1 10 units^3

2 27 units^3

11h

30 in^3

$\frac{1}{6}\text{ cm}^3$

1.435 cm^3

$\frac{1}{7}\text{ ft}$

2 cm

11i

1. Bottom: 28 ft × 14 ft
   = 392 ft^2
   Shorter sides: 6.5 ft × 14 ft
   = 91 ft^2 each so, 182 ft^2
   Longer sides = 28 ft × 6.5 ft
   = 182 ft each so, 364 ft^2

   Total square footage = 392 + 182 + 364
   = 938 ft^2
   or 938 tiles

2. Method 1:
   When pool is full, it is 6.5 ft deep,
   $\frac{3}{4}$ of $6\frac{1}{2}$ ft is $4\frac{7}{8}$ ft deep.
   So the new volume would be $14 \times 28 \times 4\frac{7}{8}$,
   which is 1,911 ft^3 or 14,103 gallons of water.

   Method 2:
   $14 \times 28 \times 6.5 = 2{,}548$ ft^3 when the pool is full.
   $2{,}548 \times \frac{3}{4} = 1{,}911$ ft^3 or 14,103 gallons of water.

11j

1. Answers vary.
2. Answers vary.

Chapter 12

12a

1. 2 : 1;
   Answers vary. Example: 4 : 2
2. 2 : 6;
   Answers vary. Example: 4 : 12
3. Answers vary. Example: 10 : 14
4. Answers vary. Example: 2 : 8
5. Answers vary. Example: 1 : 2

12b

1. 260 ÷ 5 = 52
   52 × 4 = 208
2. 52 × 2 = 104
   104 – 12 = 92

12c

1. Oranges: $0.67 per pound
   Apples: $1.10 per pound
   Grapes: $4.00 per pound
   Pineapple: $3.33 each
2. Impossible to tell as we do not know the cost of the pineapple per pound.

12d

1. Susan is right.
2. Runaway Bowling will cost $29.99 for two hours with unlimited games. This is about $10.00 per person.
   Knockem Down will cost ($2.75 x 3 people) + ($4.99 × 3 games). It equals $8.25 + $14.97 = $23.22. This is about $7.74 per person.

12e

1. 9
2. 30
3. 90
4. 400
5. 25
6. 1
7. 13.5
8. 100

12f

1. 55% + 8% + 8% + 2% = 73%
   100% – 73% = **27%**
2. Brown: 4,198,000,000
   Hazel: 611,000,000
   Blue: 611,000,000
   Green: 152,000,000
   Other: 2,061,000,000
3. Answers vary. Example:
   Because of rounding.

12g

1. Answers vary: Example:
   They all describe relationships between numbers or things.
2. Answers vary: Example:
   Ratios can describe the relationship between two separate wholes. Unit rate is a special ratio with a denominator of one. Percent is a special ratio with a denominator of 100.

3. Answers vary: Example:
Luke and Giselle mowed lawns. Giselle mowed 36 lawns and Luke mowed 24 lawns. What was the ratio of the number of lawns that Giselle mowed to the number of lawns Luke mowed? Express in simplest form.
3 : 2

4. Answers vary: Example:
It is a very fast way to see that for every 3 lawns Giselle mowed, Luke only mowed 2.

Finding the percent of lawns they mowed would have given 60% for Giselle and 40% for Luke. It is not as easy to see the relationship between the number of lawns they each mowed.

Chapter 13

13a

1. 42
3
14
2. Answers vary. Example:
It is the number that you would get if the scores were evenly distributed.

13b

1. 7
2. 5
3. 7.5
4. 1
5. 7.69
6. 3.73
7. $85 + 90 + 82 + 93 + 95 = 445$
$445 \div 5 = 89$
8. $90 \times 6 = 540.$
$540 - 445 = 95$ points

13c

1. 3
2. 3
3. 3

13d

1. 86.8 bpm; 83 bpm; 83 bpm
2. 89.7; 92; none
3. –8.3°C; –10°C; –10°C

13e

2.7; 3; none

13f

1. Answers vary. Example:
Leans to the right.
2. Answers vary. Example:
There are more scores on one side than the other or it is an uneven distribution.
3. Answers vary. Example:
Since median was higher than mean, it is not an even distribution.

13g

1. 1, 2, 3, 3, 4, **5, 5**, 5, 6, 6, 7, 7; median = 5
2. 1, 2, **3, 3**, 4, 5; median = 3
3. 5, 5, **6, 6**, 7, 7; median = 6
4. 3; 5; 6

13h

1. 11 years
2. 2.75
3. The average distance from each data point to the mean.

13i

Answers vary.

13j

1. Answers vary.
2. Answers vary.
3. Answers vary.
4. Answers vary.
5. Answers vary.

13k

1. Answers vary.
2. Answers vary.
3. Answers vary.